A TRAINER'S GUIDE TO

THE CREATIVE CURRICULUM® FOR PRESCHOOL

Candy Jones

Cate Heroman

Editor: Toni S. Bickart
Cover: Based on an original design by Kathi Dunn
Book design: Carla Uriona
Production: William A. Gordon, Jennifer Love King

Teaching Strategies, Inc.
P.O. Box 42243
Washington, DC 20015
www.TeachingStrategies.com
ISBN 13: 978-1-879537-84-2
ISBN 10: 1-879537-84-2

Library of Congress Control Number: 2003097824

Printed and bound in the United States of America
2010   2009   2008   2007   2006
10 9 8 7 6 5 4 3

Acknowledgments

We would like to thank the many dedicated teachers and administrators who attended Teaching Strategies' summer conferences in 2003 and 2004 and provided feedback on these workshop activities.

Thanks to Jan Greenberg, Sherrie Rudick, and Diane Trister Dodge for their review and comments. We appreciate Toni Bickart's editing and overall management. Thanks also to Carla Uriona and Jennifer Love King for their design and production work.

We appreciate all the early childhood educators who support teachers in making classrooms great places where young children learn and thrive as they develop language and literacy skills.

Table of Contents

Introduction

A Trainer's Guide to The Creative Curriculum® for Preschool, Volume II, "Literacy" is part of a series of guides that address content in *The Creative Curriculum*. It is a companion to *Literacy: The Creative Curriculum® Approach* and offers workshops to help teachers maximize literacy learning opportunities in their classrooms.

Across the country, expectations for children's literacy learning have been raised. Given effective instruction in the preschool years, children can meet these expectations and learn the essential literacy skills and concepts that enable them to become successful readers and writers. At Teaching Strategies, we believe that children learn these essential skills and concepts best when teachers use a comprehensive approach. This approach is described in the new supplement to *The Creative Curriculum for Preschool* called *Literacy: The Creative Curriculum Approach*.

This *Trainer's Guide* is intended for program administrators, education coordinators, and staff development specialists who are responsible for helping *Creative Curriculum* teachers learn the scope of literacy content that should be taught in their classrooms and how the research-based teaching strategies can be used to promote children's language and literacy learning and development.

How This *Trainer's Guide* Is Organized

In a *Creative Curriculum* classroom, teachers intentionally promote language and literacy learning. Their understanding of how literacy develops allows them to observe and interact with children and to evaluate children's learning. Then they can plan thoughtfully, choosing strategies to help children progress. The first step in implementing the *Creative Curriculum* approach to literacy is therefore to help teachers build their knowledge and understanding of literacy development and best practices. Part I of the *Trainer's Guide* consists of two workshop series on setting the stage for literacy learning and planning your literacy program. It presents the principles of literacy learning, the seven components of a comprehensive literacy program, and ways to create a language- and literacy-rich environment. Part II includes workshops on the seven teaching strategies: talking, singing, and playing with language; reading aloud; storytelling; story retelling; writing; supporting children's learning through play; and using studies to promote literacy.

Like Volume I, *A Trainer's Guide to The Creative Curriculum® for Preschool*, "Getting Started," each workshop series begins with an overview, stating its purpose and the big ideas that will be covered throughout the series. A chart identifies key points to be covered, the necessary materials and supplies, the pages referenced in the text, and the approximate amount of time needed for each workshop. There are page references to *Literacy: The Creative Curriculum Approach*, abbreviated as *Literacy*, and page references to *The Creative Curriculum for Preschool*, abbreviated as *Creative Curriculum*.

The instructions for each workshop have four parts. The **Preparation** section explains how to prepare for the workshop. The **Introduction** gives suggestions for introducing the workshop. The **Activity** section guides the trainer in conducting the activity. Each workshop ends with **Summary** points to be made. Handouts and transparencies are included at the end of each workshop.

Planning for Training

The workshops included in this *Trainer's Guide* mirror the content found in *Literacy: The Creative Curriculum Approach*. They are designed to be conducted in 20- to 90-minute time periods. This design allows for great flexibility in planning and scheduling. For example, training on one topic may be conducted in brief workshops over a period of time, or, workshops can be combined for lengthier training. Should a program want more in-depth study of a topic beyond the scope of the workshop, we recommend that you use one or more of the references listed in the bibliography in the Appendix of *Literacy: The Creative Curriculum Approach*.

As in Volume I of the *Trainer's Guide*, it is recommended that participants be seated at tables in groups of 6–8. This allows participants to engage in activities in different ways—with the entire group, with a partner, or alone.

As a user of this *Trainer's Guide*, remember to make these workshops your own. They provide a framework for you to present the content and big ideas presented in *Literacy: The Creative Curriculum Approach*. Before beginning training, consider the following:

- Read *Literacy: The Creative Curriculum Approach* thoroughly. As a workshop presenter, you will have more credibility if you have a thorough knowledge of the book.

- Carefully select the workshops you want to present. You may want to begin by assessing the needs and interests of the group with whom you are working. The Literacy Implementation Checklist located in the Appendix of *Literacy: The Creative Curriculum Approach* will be helpful in this process.

- Prepare ahead of time by considering ways to adapt the activities to fit your audience and training situation. For example, you may decide to read a scenario aloud to accommodate participants who read slowly, or, if time is limited, you may ask each group to respond to one question on a handout rather than all questions.

- In most workshops, we have listed "possible responses" in italics. Where they do not appear, you should prepare by recording responses you expect to hear. You should also consider any personal stories you might want to share. This is a powerful way to make people feel comfortable and more willing to share their experiences.

- The bullets suggest talking points and questions for discussion. Become familiar with them so you can use your own words.

- Make sure you have the necessary resources. Since the goal is to help participants understand the *Creative Curriculum* approach to literacy, it is recommended that each participant have a copy of *Literacy: The Creative Curriculum Approach* so they can read and refer to the book during and after the training. You will also need *The Creative Curriculum* video for select workshops.

Setting the Stage

PURPOSE

In recent years, there has been extensive research on early literacy learning. *The Creative Curriculum for Preschool* incorporates these research findings and now further expands upon them in *Literacy: The Creative Curriculum Approach*.

This workshop series on literacy begins by introducing participants to some basic principles of children's early literacy learning. Participants consider ways in which these principles impact their program practice. They examine the *Creative Curriculum* framework to learn how to use it to make important decisions about literacy content and instruction. They also begin exploring the book, *Literacy: The Creative Curriculum Approach* to see ways in which language and literacy learning can be integrated into everyday preschool experiences and activities.

In the final workshop of the series, participants learn more about each of the seven research-based components of a comprehensive literacy program as they review summaries of related research and develop understandings about the teacher's role in supporting children's development of knowledge, skills, and concepts related to each.

BIG IDEAS:

- Literacy learning begins early in children's lives.

- Literacy is best addressed as part of a comprehensive approach to curriculum and assessment for children ages 3–5.

- Literacy experience must be meaningful and purposeful for young children.

- *The Creative Curriculum for Preschool* offers teachers a framework for making decisions about children's language and literacy learning.

- Research identifies seven components of a comprehensive literacy program: literacy as a source of enjoyment; vocabulary and language; phonological awareness; knowledge of print; letters and words; comprehension; and books and other texts.

- Teachers who are knowledgeable about the components of literacy are better equipped to make informed decisions about children and daily classroom practices.

Setting the Stage

WORKSHOPS

Key Points	Workshop	Materials	Time (minutes)
Literacy learning begins early in children's lives prior to beginning school. Language and literacy experiences should be a regular, integral part of the preschool program day.	**Principles of Literacy Learning** (p. 4)	☐ Handout 3L1: Dad's Surprise Dinner ☐ Transparency 3L2: Principles of Literacy Learning	30
Reading and writing experience must be meaningful and purposeful for young children.	**Making Literacy Learning Experiences Meaningful and Purposeful** (p. 12)	☐ Chart paper, markers, crayons, construction paper, and other supplies. ☐ *Creative Curriculum*, p. 83	45
The Creative Curriculum offers teachers a framework for making decisions about children's literacy learning.	**Using the *Creative Curriculum* Framework to Plan Literacy Instruction** (p. 16)	☐ Transparency 0D: Framework ☐ Handout 0D: Framework ☐ Transparency 1D: Individual Differences ☐ *Creative Curriculum*, pp. 27–41	15–20
Knowing the seven components of literacy enables teachers to effectively teach skills and concepts children need to learn.	**The Components of Literacy** (p. 24)	☐ Handout 3L3: The Seven Components of Literacy ☐ Markers, chart paper ☐ *Literacy*, pp. 5–42	90

WORKSHOP

Principles of Literacy Learning

**Principles of Literacy
Learning**

● Literacy learning begins early
in childen's lives.

● Children's early literacy experiences
occur in real-life settings in which
they see literacy being used for
meaningful purposes.

● Adults play a key role in the
development of children's
understanding of written
language.

☐ Handout 3L1, pp. 8–9
☐ Transparency 3L2,
   pp. 10–11

◀ PREPARATION

Duplicate the handout.

Prepare the transparency.

◀ INTRODUCTION

Introduce the workshop:

- Language and literacy skills are essential for children's success
  in school and in life and the early childhood years are a critical
  period for developing these skills.

- With the increased emphasis on literacy instruction in the early
  years, this workshop series begins with an activity that asks you
  to reflect on why literacy is important and how to best nurture
  literacy learning in the early childhood classroom.

- The purpose of this workshop is to identify and discuss some
  basic principles of children's early language and literacy learning
  and to consider their implications for program practice.

◀ ACTIVITY

Distribute the handout.

Have participants read the scenario "Dad's Surprise Dinner." Ask them to
work with a partner to discuss and answer the questions on the second
page of the handout.

Review the questions and discuss participants' answers to each one.

Summarize the discussion with a review of the principles of literacy
learning. Use the transparency and the following ideas as a guide.

Explain that literacy learning begins early in children's lives:

- Many children enter school having had thousands of hours of
  literacy experiences. Parents and other family members talk with
  and read to children. Children's rooms and clothes are decorated
  with letters of the alphabet and nursery rhyme characters.
  Children experiment with writing.

- Research indicates that children who have more early literacy
  experiences have an easier time learning to read and write.

Explain that children's early literacy experiences occur in real-life settings in which they see literacy being used for meaningful purposes:

- Most of the literacy experienced by young children is embedded in familiar everyday activities such as grocery shopping, cooking, banking, eating out, or communicating with others. From these experiences, children learn that reading and writing are used to accomplish tasks. Literacy is meaningful and purposeful.

- Young children demonstrate their awareness of the purposes of print as they attempt to read print in their environment and convey meaning through their scribbles.

- In the scenario, Leo

    understood that the words his mom wrote represented the items they needed to get at the supermarket.

    knew that the list was a tool his mom used to help her remember what to buy.

    demonstrated his awareness of the meaning and purposes of print when he scribbled his own list of chocolate ice cream and sprinkles.

Explain that adults and literate others play a key role in the development of children's understanding of written language:

- As young children observe their parents, siblings, and others reading and writing, they begin to form their own notions about print.

- Young children view themselves as readers and writers. When adults talk about and involve children in literacy events and accept children's early explorations of print, regardless of the form, they convey the message that children are readers and writers.

- Through regular interactions with literate others, children continue to develop and refine their understandings of written language.

- In the scenario, Leo's Mom explained and talked aloud about what she was doing. She responded positively to Leo's request to write and accepted his scribbles as meaningful writing.

Implications for practice: Teachers must model reading and writing. They must view children as readers and writers and respond positively to their earliest efforts.

Note that, if experiences and materials are available, children's early involvement with written language is both self-initiated and self-directed:

- Children are interested in written language from an early age and take pleasure in reading and writing.

- If given the opportunity, children listen to and look at books, experiment with writing, and explore different ways to convey messages in print.

- In the scenario, Leo was curious about and expressed an interest in his Mom's writing. He initiated his writing, choosing what to write and how to write.

Implication for practice: Teachers must provide time, opportunity, and materials for children to experiment with reading and writing on their own terms and in their own way.

Talk about how reading and writing develop together and are interactive and interrelated processes:

- There has long been a notion that reading skills developed prior to writing. However, studies reveal that the two develop simultaneously.

- In the scenario, Leo's Mom named each item they needed to get from the supermarket, wrote each word, then read each word as they shopped. Leo wrote a list and read it. His mom also pretended to read his writing.

Implication for practice: Provide numerous opportunities for children to see how reading and writing work together.

◄ SUMMARY

Summarize the workshop:

- Literacy is the ability to read and write or the ability to communicate through written language.

- Children's language and literacy learning begins very early in life.

- Through their continued exposure to print through reading books and other print in the environment and writing experiences, children develop important skills and understandings that are essential to becoming successful readers.

NOTES

Dad's Surprise Dinner

Leo (3 1/2 years old) and his Mom sit snuggled in a chair reading a favorite story, *More Spaghetti, I Say!* by Rita Gelman. Leo giggles with delight as they read about Minnie's love for and adventures with spaghetti. Leo says to his Mom, "Minnie loves spaghetti as much as Dad does!" Mom smiles, then suggests to Leo that they surprise his Dad that night with a spaghetti dinner. Leo eagerly agrees. Mom tells Leo that first they will need to get a few things from the supermarket. They move to the kitchen and Leo watches as his Mom takes a small pad of paper and a pencil out of a drawer. She looks in the cupboard, then writes as she says aloud, "tomato paste, pasta, and Italian seasoning." She looks in the refrigerator and writes again.

"What are you doing, Mom?"

"I'm writing a list of the things we need to get at the supermarket to make our surprise dinner. I wouldn't want to forget anything."

Mom looks at the list, and pointing to each item says, "We'll need to remember to get tomato paste, pasta, and seasonings to make the spaghetti and sauce and lettuce, salad dressing, cheese, and croutons for the salad."

"I want to write," says Leo.

Mom replies, "OK, here is some paper and a pencil for you."

Leo sits at the table and scribbles on the paper until it's time to leave. He holds the paper tightly during the ride to the supermarket. At the store, Leo watches as his Mom reads each item on the list, puts it in the shopping cart, then crosses the item off the list.

They head towards the check-out line. Realizing they are about to leave, Leo waves the paper he has been holding. "Wait! We have to get chocolate ice cream and sprinkles," he says, pointing to the scribbles on his paper. "They're Dad's favorites!"

Mom looks at the paper. "Oh, I see—chocolate ice cream and sprinkles. It's a good thing you had your list or we wouldn't have dessert." Mom turns and heads to the frozen foods section to get the items on Leo's list.

On the way to the car Mom says, "I wonder what Dad will say about his surprise dinner?" Leo responds, "That's easy! Just like Minnie says, 'I love it, I love, I love it, I do. I love it so much'." Leo waits for his Mom to respond, "More than me?" Leo shakes his head and points to his Mom saying, "Not more than you!" They laugh together.

Dad's Surprise Dinner, continued

1. How would you define literacy?

2. What did Leo learn about literacy from this experience?

3. What roles did Leo's mother play in his literacy learning? What was her perception of Leo as a reader and writer?

4. From this scenario, what assumptions can you make about children's literacy learning?

5. How could you translate an experience such as this into practice in the preschool classroom?

Principles of Literacy Learning

- **Literacy learning begins early in childen's lives.**

- **Children's early literacy experiences occur in real-life settings in which they see literacy being used for meaningful purposes.**

- **Adults play a key role in the development of children's understanding of written language.**

● **If experiences and materials are available, children's early involvement with written language is both self-initiated and self-directed.**

● **Reading and writing develop together. They are interactive and interrelated processes.**

WORKSHOP

Making Literacy Learning Experiences Meaningful and Purposeful

☐ Chart paper, markers, crayons, construction paper, and other supplies

☐ *Creative Curriculum*, p. 83

PREPARATION

Set up activity stations as described so that participants can visit each one.

Station 1: Set up a check in and/or sign in area similar to one described for the preschool classroom on page 83 of *The Creative Curriculum*. If participants have to check in, secure a list of names ahead of time to so you can prepare name cards.

Station 2: Purchase or make a graphing grid and post it on the wall. At the top write *How many years have you been teaching?* Label each column as follows: 0–5, 6–10, 11–15, 16–20, 21–25, 26+. Provide squares of colored paper and tape, colored adhesive dots, and markers so participants can choose how to indicate their responses on the graph.

Station 3: On chart paper, write the caption *What do you hope to learn today?* Provide markers so participants can respond in writing.

Station 4: Write the question, Do you like to read? at the top of a piece of chart paper. Draw a line down the middle of the chart paper to create two columns. Label one column Yes and the other column No. Have the participants sign their names in the appropriate column.

Station 5: Use environmental print (food packages) to create a picture/word recipe for Trail Mix found in *The Trainer's Guide to The Creative Curriculum for Preschool*. Provide the ingredients for participants to make a snack.

Trail Mix (single Serving)	
Food: 1/4 cup each Chex cereals (corn, wheat, rice) 1/4 cup Cherrios 10 pretzel sticks 1–2 teaspoons raisins 1 tablespoon shredded coconut slivered almonds (optional)	*Method:* Measure the ingredients and place into a baggie.

Station 6: On chart paper, pose a question such as the ones that follow. Provide paper and markers or crayons so participants can respond. Prior to the workshop, make a book cover appropriate for the topic you selected. After participants complete their writing, combine the pages to form a book.

- It's been said that there is a pot of gold at the end of every rainbow. If you found that pot of gold, what would you do with it? Draw and write about it.

- You have won an all-expense-paid trip for two to any place in the world you choose. Where would you go and why? Who would you take with you? Write and draw about your trip.

Station 7: Create a job or helper chart for the workshop as teachers might do in the classroom and post it at the station. The jobs might include giving a summary report of the information at one of the stations, reading or sharing a thought for the day, passing out workshop materials, reading the break/lunch menu, or reading a few pages from the book created by the group. Write instructions so participants who have assigned jobs will know what to do.

Prepare an agenda for the workshop. Duplicate it for each participant or post it in the training room so all participants can see it clearly.

Write a message on chart paper welcoming participants to the workshop, introducing yourself (if you are a trainer from outside the organization), and instructing them to proceed to the stations. Note that when they are finished working at the stations, they may return to a table. Position the message so participants will see it on their way into the training room.

Make yourself available to those participants who arrive late or have questions. Allow approximately 30 minutes for participants to complete the work at the stations.

INTRODUCTION

As participants enter, encourage them to begin work as indicated on the agenda.

After everyone has finished work at the stations, bring the group together.

Review the agenda. Refer to the agenda, modeling the way a teacher might use the daily schedule to let children know about the day's events.

Debrief the stations work with the following points:

- Literacy is an important part of everyday life. It is a tool we use regularly to accomplish many and varied tasks.

- One of the main goals in the early childhood classroom is to help children understand the functions and value of print.

- The purpose of this workshop is to examine ways in which reading and writing experiences can be made meaningful and purposeful for children.

◀ ACTIVITY

Refer to the job chart from station 7, asking each of the assigned participants to give a report or read a few selected pages from the group's book.

Have participants reflect on the literacy experiences at the stations. Recall that in a previous workshop they defined literacy. Lead a discussion about the types of literacy experiences that should be offered in the preschool classroom. Use the following questions to guide the discussion.

• Could you have completed the tasks if you could not read or write? Why is it essential for children to learn to read and write?

Possible responses:

Reading and writing are skills essential for life.

They enable us to

> *communicate with others*

> *acquire information*

> *share our thoughts and ideas*

> *reflect our identity*

> *express ourselves creatively*

> *find out how to do something (follow directions)*

• How would you describe the station activities? What characteristics come to mind?

Possible responses:

Personal

Real or authentic

Purposeful (to learn about the participants in the workshop)

Involved both reading and writing

Participants could respond in their own ways

- What are the implications for classroom practice?

Possible responses:

*Children should have opportunities to participate in a variety of meaningful **reading** and **writing** experiences.*

Literacy experiences should reflect the many functions or purposes of print.

Children will communicate in a variety of ways (as participants did in their responses; they could use colored squares, dots, or markers to reflect their years of teaching experience).

◀ SUMMARY

Summarize the workshop:

- Reading and writing experiences should be meaningful for children; they should serve a purpose.

- Through such experiences, children learn that written language is a tool that they can use to communicate messages, learn new information and concepts, organize and express their thoughts, care for the classroom and the environment, and know what to do.

Using the *Creative Curriculum* Framework to Plan Literacy Instruction

☐ Transparency 0D, p. 22
☐ Handout 0D, p. 22
☐ Transparency 1D, p. 23
☐ *Creative Curriculum,*
   pp. 27–41

◖ **PREPARATION**

Prepare the transparencies. Duplicate the handout.

◖ **INTRODUCTION**

Introduce the workshop:

- With the increased emphasis on literacy in the early years and in an effort to comply with federal mandates, some programs have set aside their comprehensive curriculum and replaced it with a "literacy only" curriculum.

- Others use a curriculum intended for older children or insert literacy into an existing curriculum with specific times of the day set aside for teaching literacy skills.

- Neither of these approaches is the best way to ensure that children acquire a solid foundation in language and literacy.

- Literacy instruction is most effective when it is built into a comprehensive approach that gives equal attention to all aspects of a child's development—social and emotional, physical, cognitive, and language development.

- There are times for direct teaching—one-on-one, in small groups, and in large groups—and there are times for children to explore and experiment with language and literacy on their own.

- *Literacy: The Creative Curriculum Approach*, a supplement to *The Creative Curriculum for Preschool*, is based on the latest reading research and research-based teaching strategies. It reflects the belief that literacy develops best when it is infused into every aspect of the day.

- Take a few minutes to browse through the book.

Close this introduction by asking participants to comment on what they noticed.

◀ ACTIVITY

Show transparency 0D. Use the points below to describe how the *Creative Curriculum* framework is used to make decisions about language and literacy instruction. Participants may wish to take notes on handout 0D.

Research

- *The Creative Curriculum* rests on a foundation of research and theory including the work of Piaget, Maslow, Erikson, Smilansky, Vygotsky, and Gardner as well as the latest research about learning, the brain, and resiliency.

- In recent years, other research and reports have been published which have expanded our understanding of how children develop and learn and outlined ways to address academic content with preschool children.

- We know that literacy skills are learned—they don't just happen.

- Teachers need to plan literacy experiences intentionally.

- Young children need to be challenged to the edge of their competencies.

- General knowledge, skills, and attitudes play important roles in early literacy development.

- You will see these points reflected throughout *Literacy: The Creative Curriculum Approach*.

How Children Develop and Learn

- Teaching begins with knowing children—what they are like and how they learn, both developmentally and individually.

- Teachers use their knowledge of child development to make decisions about how to best promote children's language and literacy learning.

- Teachers can use this knowledge to guide them in making decisions about all aspects of their programs: the arrangement of the physical environment, the design of the daily schedule, and topics of study.

Ask participants to give examples of what preschool children are like.

Possible responses:

active	*curious about their world*
love to talk	*like to play*
explore using senses	*feel competent*
developing small muscles	*like to do things on their own*
can't sit still for long periods of time	

Choose one characteristic and ask participants how it would influence their literacy practice. For example, knowing that preschool children *like to play and explore*:

- A teacher would encourage children to play or experiment with language.

- A teacher would incorporate literacy materials into interest areas so the children can use them in their own way during play.

Show transparency 1D and review the individual differences described in *The Creative Curriculum for Preschool*, pp. 27–41.

Have participants choose one individual difference and talk with a partner about how they could use that information to promote a child's language and literacy learning.

- For example, what would you do with a child who is slow to warm up or approaches new situations slowly and cautiously?

  Possible responses:

  Share a book with the child individually or in a small group prior to reading it with a large group of children.

  Pair the child with one who is more social.

  Offer language and literacy activities and experiences in small group settings.

  Establish and follow regular routines so the child will feel confident that she knows when and what to do (e.g., put in place a daily sign-in procedure or schedule storytime at the same time each day).

The Learning Environment

- The learning environment is the starting point for implementing *The Creative Curriculum*.

- This component addresses how teachers set up and maintain the physical environment, establish a structure for the day, and create a classroom community.

- *Literacy: The Creative Curriculum Approach* gives teachers guidance about how to create a language- and literacy-rich environment and how to incorporate literacy into every event of the day in meaningful ways.

What Children Learn

- There are seven components of literacy described in *The Creative Curriculum* and expanded upon in *Literacy: The Creative Curriculum Approach*. They include:

    literacy as a source of enjoyment

    vocabulary and language

    phonological awareness

    knowledge of print

    letters and words

    comprehension

    books and other texts

- These components are based on the research describing a comprehensive literacy program.

- The first step in implementing a literacy program is to become knowledgeable about these components of literacy.

The Teacher's Role

- Some children enter school with early reading and writing skills, while others have very limited experiences.

- A teacher's first job is to **observe** in order to find out what children know and can do. Then the teacher can respond appropriately and plan instruction.

- Teachers **guide** children's language and literacy learning using a range of instructional approaches. *Literacy: The Creative Curriculum Approach* describes seven essential early literacy teaching strategies appropriate for use in the preschool classroom. They include:

    talking, singing, and playing with language

    reading aloud

    storytelling

    story retelling

    writing

    playing: children's work

    studies: using literacy to learn

- Sometimes the strategies are part of planned activities used at particular times of the day. At other times teachers use the strategies more spontaneously to extend learning while interacting with children in interest areas.

- Teaching and assessing go hand in hand. The language section of *The Creative Curriculum Developmental Continuum* describes the sequence of developmental steps children typically demonstrate as they master each of the 13 language objectives.

- Through assessment, teachers gather information about children in order to make instructional decisions that support their language and literacy learning.

The Family's Role

- Language and literacy experiences begin at birth, and family members are children's first and life-long teachers.

- Through partnerships, families and teachers can work together to foster children's literacy learning.

The Interest Areas

- Children spend a significant part of each day in child-initiated play in interest areas.

- When each area is organized with literacy in mind, children's time is well spent and literacy learning is maximized.

- Chapter 4 of *Literacy: The Creative Curriculum Approach* describes how teachers can make each interest area a valuable place for literacy learning and how they can interact with children in ways that promote each component of literacy.

◀ SUMMARY

Summarize the workshop:

- *The Creative Curriculum* is a blueprint for planning and implementing a developmentally appropriate program.

- Its framework serves as a tool for making decisions about literacy instruction as well as other aspects of the program.

NOTES

Framework

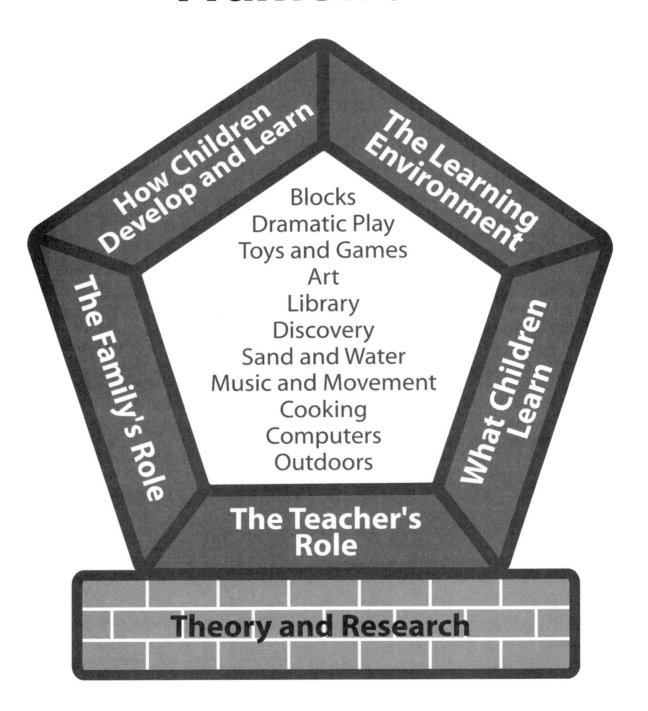

How Children Develop and Learn

The Learning Environment

The Family's Role

What Children Learn

Blocks
Dramatic Play
Toys and Games
Art
Library
Discovery
Sand and Water
Music and Movement
Cooking
Computers
Outdoors

The Teacher's Role

Theory and Research

OD

Individual Differences

- **Gender**

- **Temperament**

- **Interests**

- **Learning Style**

- **Life Experiences**

- **Culture**

- **Special Needs**

- **Second Language Learners**

1D

The Components of Literacy

☐ Handout 3L3, p. 27
☐ Markers, chart paper
☐ *Literacy*, pp. 5–42

PREPARATION

Duplicate the handout.

Think of a way to assign one of the components to each small group for study.

INTRODUCTION

Introduce the workshop:

- Research on early literacy learning and instruction describes the essential elements of a comprehensive literacy program.

- These elements are referred to as the components of literacy and are described in Chapter 1 of *Literacy: The Creative Curriculum Approach*. They include:

  literacy as a source of enjoyment

  vocabulary and language

  phonological awareness

  knowledge of print

  letters and words

  comprehension

  books and other texts

- Teachers who understand each of the components are able to identify children's needs and plan daily classroom experiences that promote literacy learning.

- The purposes of this workshop are to introduce these seven components of literacy and the related research, and discuss the teacher's role in supporting the development of skills and concepts related to each of the components.

ACTIVITY

Have participants form seven groups. Use the system you have devised so that each group knows which one of the components they are to discuss.

Explain that they will read the section in the book (pp. 5–42) that describes the component of literacy assigned to their group. They will talk among themselves to share what they have learned about the particular component.

Their next task will be to design a way to present the key points of information about the component to the rest of the participants. Each group's presentation should last no longer than five minutes. They should try to present the information in a way that will help others remember it.

Before the groups begin their work, ask them to think of strategies they use to help them to remember information. Record their ideas on a chart so that they can use these ideas as they design their presentations.

Possible responses:

music/song

visuals

role-play or dramatization

first-hand experience or participation

acrostic

Suggest that the groups use one or more of these strategies when they present the information on their component to the rest of the participants.

Allow about 30 minutes for the groups to work.

Distribute the handout and explain that it can be used to take notes during the presentations.

Ask groups to present. Provide additional information or comments as needed.

◀ SUMMARY

Summarize the workshop:

- Knowing the components of literacy helps teachers to plan a comprehensive literacy program.

- This information is the basis for the intentional teaching strategies and activities teachers will use to help children become competent and confident readers and writers.

◀ VARIATION

Have participants form seven groups. Assign one component to each group and explain that they will be considered the "experts" on the assigned component.

Have participants read the appropriate section in *Literacy: The Creative Curriculum Approach* (pp. 5–42) and then talk among themselves to share what they have learned. Suggest that they make notes on the handout so that they can share their expertise with others.

Allow 20 minutes for groups to meet.

Have participants form new groups making sure that each of the components is represented in the new groups.

Have each of the "experts" share what they have learned with others in their new group. They can record their ideas on the handout.

The Seven Components of Literacy

Components	Notes
Literacy as a Source of Enjoyment	
Vocabulary and Language	
Phonological Awareness	
Knowledge of Print	
Letters and Words	
Comprehension	
Books and Other Texts	

Planning Your Literacy Program

PURPOSE

The learning environment is the starting point for implementing *The Creative Curriculum for Preschool*. The physical space sets the stage for learning and affects children's behavior. The daily routines and schedule bring order to the day and help children to function as a group. In a classroom that functions as a community, there is a positive social climate that encourages conversations. Given the importance of the learning environment, *Literacy: The Creative Curriculum Approach* explains how the physical design of the classroom can contribute to children's language and literacy development and how literacy can become a regular, integral part of children's daily experiences.

In this workshop series, participants learn how to create a language- and literacy-rich environment where children have opportunities to use and see adults use reading and writing in meaningful and functional ways from the time they arrive until they leave for the day. Participants will also have the opportunity to assess their environment using the Literacy Implementation Checklist.

BIG IDEAS:

- Literacy should be an integral part of children's everyday experiences.

- A carefully planned environment can support children's language and literacy development.

- Teachers should provide opportunities for children to use and see adults use reading and writing in meaningful, functional ways throughout the day.

- The Literacy Implementation Checklist is a useful tool for assessing the literacy environment in a *Creative Curriculum* classroom.

Planning Your Literacy Program

WORKSHOPS

🔑 Key Points	⚙ Workshop	📋 Materials	🕐 Time (minutes)
Literacy should be a natural and integral part of everyday events.	**Creating a Language- and Literacy-Rich Environment** (p. 32)	☐ *Literacy*, pp.53–56 and Chapter 4 ☐ Handout 3L4: Incorporating Language and Literacy Into the Daily Schedule	60–90
Environments that nourish early literacy are rich with materials for reading and writing.	**Assessing Your Literacy Program** (p. 36)	☐ Handout 3L5: Literacy Implementation Checklist ☐ Handout 3L6: Literacy Implementation Checklist: Self-Assessment Summary ☐ Variation–Photos or slides illustrating the items in the Literacy Implementation Checklist	30

WORKSHOP

Creating a Language- and Literacy-Rich Environment

☐ Handout 3L4, p. 35
☐ *Literacy*, pp. 53–56 and Chapter 4

◖ PREPARATION

Duplicate the handout.

◖ INTRODUCTION

Ask participants to think about all of the literacy experiences (reading and writing) they have had since they arose that morning.

Allow a few minutes for discussion at tables. Then ask the group members to share their ideas as you record them on a chart or transparency.

Ask:

• What observations can you make about the role of literacy (reading and writing) in your everyday life?

Possible responses:

Literacy is an integral part of our daily lives.

Reading and writing are essential, life-long skills.

Reading and writing are important tools for communication.

Written language provides information, tells people what or how to do something, is a means through which we entertain others or express our thoughts, ideas, and opinions.

Print is all around us. It is used to label and organize the environment.

Print helps us to remember or recall information.

• What would your daily life be like without written language?

Possible responses:

It would be less organized.

It would be chaotic or hectic.

I would rely more heavily upon others.

I would be dependent on oral language, therefore those skills would need to be more refined.

Go back through the list and draw parallels between some of the items listed and the classroom environment.

Make the following points:

- Written language is an integral part of our daily lives. Therefore, reading and writing skills are necessary skills for daily living and essential for life-long learning.

- The purpose of this workshop is to explore ways in which reading and writing experiences can be integrated into the learning environment to promote children's literacy development.

ACTIVITY

Have participants list the important language and literacy skills and habits they would like to see children learn and demonstrate. Then have them identify when and where they could provide opportunities for children to cultivate these skills and habits.

Invite participants to share their ideas. Then make the following points:

- The learning environment is the "textbook" in a *Creative Curriculum* classroom. It includes the physical setting, the program structure, and the social climate.

- During this activity, you will consider ways in which the physical environment and the daily schedule can be designed to promote language and literacy development.

Have participants at each table form two groups. Give the following instructions:

- Group 1 at each table:

  Generate a list of ways the **physical environment** can be designed to promote oral language, reading, and writing. Think carefully about the overall environment as well as different interest areas.

- Group 2 at each table:

  Generate a list of ways teachers can promote oral **language, reading, and writing throughout the day,** such as arrival and departure, attendance, group times, meal and snack time, choice time, outdoors, and routines.

Have the groups exchange ideas at their tables or invite each small group to share one or two ideas alternately with the whole group.

Refer participants to pages 53–56 in *Literacy: The Creative Curriculum Approach*. Review any items not covered in your discussion.

Have participants take a mental tour of their classrooms, making note of print they have displayed in the environment.

Ask them to consider these points:

- Determine whether the print serves a purpose and should remain on display.

- Identify other opportunities to integrate print in meaningful ways.

Refer participants to the charts of suggested materials and books found in Chapter 4 of *Literacy: The Creative Curriculum Approach*.

Next, distribute the handout. Explain to participants that they are to think about their daily schedule and routines to determine if they adequately address the language and literacy needs of their children. Give the following instructions:

- List each day's events in column one.

- In column two, record the oral language, reading, and writing experiences you currently offer to children during this event. They may be child-initiated or teacher-initiated.

- In column three, list other oral language, reading, and writing experiences you would like to try based on the ideas you have heard during our discussion today.

SUMMARY

Summarize the workshop:

- The learning environment is the starting point for implementing *The Creative Curriculum*.

- When the physical environment is arranged effectively and interest areas are well-equipped with reading and writing materials that address the needs and interests of the children, language and literacy opportunities flourish.

- In a *Creative Curriculum* classroom, every event of the day is an opportunity for literacy learning.

Incorporating Language and Literacy Into the Daily Schedule

Event of the Day	Language and Literacy Experiences I Currently Offer	Language and Literacy Experiences I Am Going to Offer
Arrival		
Attendance		
Large-Group Time		
Small-Group Time		
Meal and Snack Time		
Choice Time		
Outdoors		
Routines		
Transitions		
Departure		

Assessing Your Literacy Program

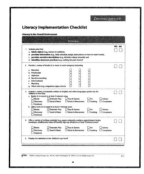

☐ Handout 3L5, pp. 38–40
☐ Handout 3L6, p. 41

◀ PREPARATION

Duplicate the handouts.

Distribute handout 3L5 prior to the workshop and have participants complete a self-assessment. Ask them to bring the completed handout to the workshop.

◀ INTRODUCTION

Introduce the workshop:

• The Literacy Implementation Checklist is an expanded version of the literacy sections from *The Creative Curriculum for Preschool Implementation Checklist*, a tool designed to help you determine the degree to which you are implementing *The Creative Curriculum for Preschool*.

• You can find this Literacy Implementation Checklist in the Appendix of the *Literacy: The Creative Curriculum Approach*. The handout you completed prior to coming to this workshop is a copy of what is in the Appendix.

• The purposes of this workshop are to discuss and clarify any items or terms you have questions about, to reflect on the results of your self-assessment, and to develop a plan for strengthening your literacy program.

• You have probably discovered that you already meet many of the criteria on the Checklist. Now you can focus attention on areas that need strengthening.

◀ ACTIVITY

Have participants take out the self-assessment they completed prior to the workshop.

Discuss each of the following sections of the Checklist:

1. Literacy in the Overall Environment

2. Literacy in the Library Area

3. Guiding Children's Literacy Learning

Clarify any items or terminology about which the group has questions.

Distribute handout 3L6. Then give the following instructions:

- Review your self-assessment. Determine your areas of strength and identify areas in which you would like to improve. Record your ideas in the appropriate space on the handout.

- Partner with someone at your table. Take turns discussing your findings. Talk about specific steps you will take to strengthen your literacy environment and the ways in which you guide children's literacy learning.

- Invite your partner to offer suggestions.

SUMMARY

Summarize the workshop:

- The Literacy Implementation Checklist gives you a quick way to assess the literacy environment in your classroom.

- It offers guidance on ways in which the classroom can be organized and equipped so that optimal language and literacy development can occur.

- It helps you think about how much you are addressing skills and concepts as you use the teaching strategies.

VARIATION

Display photos of classroom environments.

Have participants rate the environments using the first two pages of the Literacy Implementation Checklist.

Have participants form small groups to discuss their results, summarizing each classroom's strengths and areas needing improvement.

Literacy Implementation Checklist

Literacy in the Overall Environment

Do Teachers	YES	NO

1. Include print that
    a. **labels objects** (e.g., names on cubbies),
    b. **provides information** (e.g., daily schedule, recipe, instructions on how to wash hands),
    c. **provides narrative descriptions** (e.g., dictation about artwork), and
    d. **identifies classroom practices** (e.g., waiting lists, job charts)?
	☐	☐

2. Provide a variety of books (3 or more in each category) including
 	
    a. Narrative ☐ ☐ ☐
    b. Predictable ☐ ☐ ☐
    c. Alphabet ☐ ☐ ☐
    d. Number/counting ☐ ☐ ☐
    e. Informational ☐ ☐ ☐
    f. Rhyming ☐ ☐ ☐
    g. Other texts (e.g., magazines, signs, charts) ☐ ☐ ☐
	☐	☐

3. Include a variety of materials written in English and other languages spoken by the children in the class:
    a. Books (3 or more) in at least 5 interest areas
      ☐ Blocks ☐ Dramatic Play ☐ Toys & Games ☐ Art ☐ Library
      ☐ Discovery ☐ Sand & Water ☐ Music & Movement ☐ Cooking ☐ Computers
      ☐ Outdoors
    b. Other texts (3 or more) in at least 3 interest areas
      ☐ Blocks ☐ Dramatic Play ☐ Toys & Games ☐ Art ☐ Library
      ☐ Discovery ☐ Sand & Water ☐ Music & Movement ☐ Cooking ☐ Computers
      ☐ Outdoors
	☐	☐

4. Offer a variety of writing materials (e.g., paper, notepads, markers, appointment books, envelopes, chalkboards, wipe-off boards, sign-up sheets) in at least 5 interest areas?
 	
    ☐ Blocks ☐ Dramatic Play ☐ Toys & Games ☐ Art ☐ Library
    ☐ Discovery ☐ Sand & Water ☐ Music & Movement ☐ Cooking ☐ Computers
    ☐ Outdoors
	☐	☐

5. Display the alphabet at the children's eye level?	☐	☐

From *Literacy: The Creative Curriculum® Approach*
©2005 Teaching Strategies, Inc., PO Box 42243, Washington, DC 20015; www.TeachingStrategies.com

3L5

Literacy Implementation Checklist, continued

Literacy in the Library Area

	Do Teachers	YES	NO
1.	Make the Library Area available as a choice activity on a daily basis?	☐	☐

2.	Provide a variety of materials and furnishings to make the space comfortable and attractive (e.g., carpeted floor, good lighting, beanbag chairs, child-size rocker) where children can look at books?
	  a. Feature #1: _____
	  b. Feature #2: _____
	  c. Feature #3: _____
		☐	☐

3.	Provide space and materials for listening (e.g., books stored together with tapes or CDs, cassette recorder or CD players, two headphones)?	☐	☐

4.	Include a
	  a. Bookshelf to display books facing out?
	  b. Table and chairs for writing?
	  c. Shelf for writing materials?
		☐	☐

5.	Provide a variety of materials to
	  a. **Write on** (e.g., assorted lined and unlined paper, chalkboards, envelopes, stationery)
	    1) _____
	    2) _____
	    3) _____
	  b. **Write with** (e.g., pencils, pens, markers, chalk)
	    1) _____
	    2) _____
	    3) _____
	  c. **Letter and Word Manipulatives** (e.g., letter stamps, name cards, alphabet cards for children to handle and use as models)?
	    1) _____
	    2) _____
	    3) _____
		☐	☐

6.	Display (with covers facing out) at least 25 children's books (e.g., storybooks; nursery rhymes; and informational, predictable, alphabet, and number/counting books)?	☐	☐
7.	Provide books and related props for retelling stories (e.g., hand puppets, flannel board, magnetic board, or story apron related to a particular story?)	☐	☐

Teaching Strategies. From *Literacy: The Creative Curriculum® Approach*
©2005 Teaching Strategies, Inc., PO Box 42243, Washington, DC 20015; www.TeachingStrategies.com

3L5

Literacy Implementation Checklist, continued

Guiding Children's Literacy Learning

Do Teachers	YES	NO
1. Read books to individuals as well as to large and small groups at least twice every day, and prompt children to interact and respond (e.g., take a picture walk through the story before reading, leave out a word so children can fill it in, ask open-ended questions, relate the story to prior experiences)?	☐	☐
2. Engage children in retelling a story using puppets, flannel board figures, or props?	☐	☐
3. Draw children's attention to the sounds of language through playful songs, stories, rhymes, and chants to help develop **phonological awareness**?	☐	☐
4. Draw children's attention to a. **concepts of print** (e.g., left to right, top to bottom) and b. **concepts of books** (e.g., author, illustrator, book-handling skills, turning pages)?	☐	☐
5. Draw children's attention to **letters and words** (e.g., reading big books and pointing to words, taking a walk to look for signs, writing a group thank-you letter)?	☐	☐
6. **Talk with children** throughout the day, **modeling correct grammar, introducing new vocabulary** and **asking questions** to encourage children to express their ideas in words?	☐	☐
7. **Write with children** (e.g., record their ideas and stories, write experience charts, write a thank you note to a visitor) and **encourage children to write** (e.g., put their names on artwork, create a shopping list in dramatic play, make signs for a block structure)?	☐	☐

Literacy Implementation Checklist:
Self-Assessment Summary

What areas are well-established?

What areas need improvement?

Steps I plan to take to enrich my literacy environment:

3L6

Teaching Strategies

PURPOSE

With an understanding of the components of literacy, a teacher's next step is to plan ways to support children's literacy learning. *Literacy: The Creative Curriculum Approach* describes seven appropriate teaching strategies that can be used to address a program's language and literacy goals for children. They include talking, singing, and playing with language; reading aloud; storytelling; story retelling; writing; supporting children's learning through play; and using studies to promote literacy.

Participants will be familiar with some of these strategies; however, during this workshop series, they will explore ways in which these strategies are used most effectively so that children's learning is maximized.

BIG IDEAS:

- A strong foundation in oral language contributes significantly to children's literacy development.

- Reading aloud is the most powerful teaching strategy. It helps to instill a love for books and reading and helps children to learn many important literacy skills and concepts.

- Everyone is a storyteller, children as well as adults. *Creative Curriculum* teachers should offer children opportunities to tell stories regularly—personal, real-life stories as well as those that have been read or told by teachers and family members.

- Story retelling is one of the most effective strategies for developing children's comprehension and understanding of story structure.

- Reading and writing are interactive and interrelated processes. Therefore, writing should be an integral part of the preschool program.

- Play is an effective vehicle for learning language and literacy skills and concepts.

- Studies provide a way to learn literacy skills in a context that is meaningful and engaging.

Talking, Singing, and Playing With Language

WORKSHOPS

🔑 Key Points	⚙ Workshop	🗐 Materials	🕐 Time (minutes)
A strong foundation in oral language contributes significantly to children's literacy development.	**Oral Language Development** (p. 46)	☐ Transparency 3L7: Keys to Future Success as Readers and Writers ☐ Transparency 3L8: What Is Language? ☐ Transparency 3L9: Rules of Language ☐ Transparency 3L10: The Link Between Language and Literacy ☐ Transparency 3L11: English Language Learners ☐ Transparency 3L12: *Creative Curriculum* Teachers… ☐ Transparency 3L13: Planned Oral Language Experiences ☐ Variation–Props, pictures	10–15
Firsthand experiences enable children to develop concepts, acquire knowledge, and learn new vocabulary. This knowledge base is essential for comprehending what is read.	**Promoting Language and Literacy Through Firsthand Experiences** (p. 56)	☐ Materials: objects to explore, replica of objects, black line drawing of objects, name of objects written on paper ☐ Handout 3L14: Learning Language Through Firsthand Experiences	30
Conversations with children are an important way to promote cognitive, social/emotional, and language development.	**Facilitating Conversations** (p. 60)	☐ Handout 4E: Responding to Children—Scenarios ☐ Handout 3L15: Facilitating Conversation ☐ Variations–Props, pictures	30
Teachers use songs, rhymes, and other language games to teach essential literacy skills intentionally.	**Using Songs, Rhymes, and Other Language Play Activities** (p. 68)	☐ Bumble bee puppet ☐ Materials for small-group work based on selected activities from *Literacy*, chapter 5	45

WORKSHOP

Oral Language Development

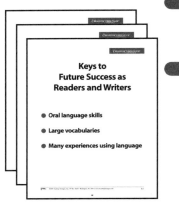

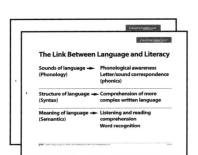

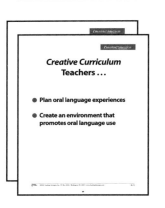

PREPARATION

Prepare the transparencies.

INTRODUCTION

Introduce workshop:

- The first teaching strategy described in *Literacy: The Creative Curriculum Approach* is Talking, Singing, and Playing With Language.

- We begin with this strategy since oral language is the foundation of children's later literacy learning.

ACTIVITY

Pose the following question, and then have participants discuss their thoughts with others at their tables:

- Why is oral language development important during the preschool years?

Invite participants to share key points from their discussions.

Use the transparencies and the points below as a guide to summarize the discussion.

Transparency 3L7: Keys to Future Success as Readers and Writers

- Research tells us that children's oral language skills during the preschool years are strong predictors of their future success as readers and writers.

- Children who have large vocabularies and lots of experience using language are more successful in school.

- For these reasons, one of the main goals of preschool programs should be to ensure that children have a firm foundation in oral language.

Transparency 3L8: What Is Language?

- Learning language involves learning a set of language systems each with its own rules.

- In order to communicate your thoughts, ideas, and feelings to others and to understand others thoughts, ideas, and feelings, everyone has to have a clear understanding of the rules.

Transparency 3L9: Rules of Language?

- There are rules that govern the sounds of language (referred to as phonology). Children must learn about the 44 separate sounds or phonemes, pitch (high/low voice), stress (how loud or soft a sound is), juncture (pauses and connections between words, phrases, and sentences). Read some of the following sentences as examples.

    When shot at, the dove dove into the bushes.
    The farm was used to produce produce.
    The soldier decided to desert his unit in the desert, after eating dessert.
    The wind is too strong to wind the sail.

- There are rules that govern the structure of language (referred to as syntax). Children must learn how words work together to form phrases, clauses, and sentences.

- There are rules about the meaning that language communicates (referred to as semantics). These govern vocabulary development.

Read an excerpt from *The King Who Rained* or *A Chocolate Moose for Dinner* by Fred Gwynne or *Cook-A-Doodle-Doo* by Janet Stevens and Susan Stevens Crummel as an example.

Transparency 3L10: The Link Between Language and Literacy

- Children who have a better understanding of the rules of oral language have an easier time applying those rules to written language.

Transparency 3L11: English Language Learners

Transparency 3L12: *Creative Curriculum* Teachers...

- In a *Creative Curriculum* classroom, teachers promote children's oral language development in two ways. They intentionally

    plan oral language experiences
    create an environment that promotes oral language use

Transparency 3L13: Planned Oral language Experience

- *Literacy: The Creative Curriculum Approach* describes three types of planned experiences teachers use to promote children's oral language development:

    firsthand experiences
    conversations
    songs, rhymes, and language games

- You will explore each of these experiences and learn how they address the key components of literacy.

SUMMARY

Summarize the workshop:

- Oral language is the basis for the development of reading and writing.

- As children engage in oral language experiences, they learn new vocabulary and about the way in which language is structured.

- Children who have a solid understanding of oral language, can more easily transfer what they know to written language.

Keys to Future Success as Readers and Writers

- **Oral language skills**

- **Large vocabularies**

- **Many experiences using language**

What Is Language?

Language is a system of words with rules for their use in speaking, reading, and writing.

Rules of Language

- **Sounds of language (Phonology)**

- **Structure of language (Syntax)**

- **Meaning of language (Semantics)**

The Link Between Language and Literacy

Sounds of language ➞ **Phonological awareness**
(Phonology)   **Letter/sound correspondence**
                                         (phonics)

Structure of language ➞ **Comprehension of more**
(Syntax)   **complex written language**

Meaning of language ➞ **Listening and reading**
(Semantics)   **comprehension**
                                       Word recognition

English Language Learners

● A strong base in a first language promotes school achievement in a second language.

● English language learners are more likely to become readers and writers of English if they are already familiar with the vocabulary and concepts in their primary language.

©2005 Teaching Strategies, Inc., PO Box 42243, Washington, DC 20015; www.TeachingStrategies.com

Creative Curriculum Teachers . . .

- **Plan oral language experiences**

- **Create an environment that promotes oral language use**

Planned Oral Language Experiences

- **Firsthand experiences**

- **Conversations**

- **Songs, rhymes, and other playful language games**

Promoting Language and Literacy Through Firsthand Experiences

☐ Handout 3L14, p. 59

● PREPARATION

Duplicate the handout.

Gather and prepare these materials:

1. real objects, one for each participant or pair of participants to explore (e.g., flowers, apples, nuts, or shells plus tools such as plastic knives, magnifying glasses, reflective paper, nut crackers)
2. one replica of the real object for each table (e.g., artificial flower, plastic fruit)
3. one black-line drawing of the object, large enough for the entire group to see clearly
4. the name of the object written on a piece of paper, large enough for the entire group to read

● INTRODUCTION

Introduce the workshop:

- From theorists such as Piaget and Vygotsky, we learned that children construct their own understanding of the world as they manipulate objects, participate in firsthand experiences, and interact with knowledgeable peers and adults.

- In this activity, you will focus on how firsthand experiences contribute specifically to children's literacy learning.

● ACTIVITY

Distribute the handout. Explain to participants that they will complete the handout as they engage in four rounds of exploration of a familiar object. Follow the procedures below.

Exploration 1:
Give each participant or each pair of participants one of the real objects. Have them explore the object, learning as much as they can about it. Tell them they may use all of their senses and any of the tools on the table during their explorations. Have them list words to describe what they learned about their object in section 1 of the handout.

Exploration 2:
Give each table the replica of the real object. Have them each quickly explore it then pass it to the person next to them. Have them list words to describe what they learned about the object in section 2 of the handout.

Exploration 3:
Show the line drawing of the object. Have participants explore the object as you walk about. Have them list words to describe what they learned about the object in section 3 of the handout.

Exploration 4:
Show the paper with the word of the object. Have participants explore the word as you walk about. Have them list words to describe what they learned about the object in section 4 of the handout.

Invite participants to share their observations about the experience. Ask:

- What can you conclude about firsthand experiences after doing this activity?

- How do they contribute to children's language and literacy development?

  Possible responses:

  Children's vocabularies are greatly expanded through firsthand experiences.

  The more senses involved in the exploration, the greater the increase in vocabulary.

  Language is enriched as a result of the interactions (conversations and exchange of ideas) between peers.

  Children are more likely to develop new concepts and their knowledge base is increased as a result of firsthand experiences with real objects. This will improve comprehension.

  The amount of time and the tools available affect the quality of children's language and learning.

SUMMARY

Summarize the workshop:

- Children's thinking changes over time moving from the concrete to the abstract.

- Through firsthand experiences, children develop concepts, acquire background knowledge, and learn new vocabulary which they will need to comprehend what they read.

- Therefore, early childhood programs should offer children many and repeated firsthand experiences.

- It is important to remember that teachers need to be part of these experiences to talk with children, ask questions, and extend learning. We'll be considering the teacher's role in later workshops.

NOTES

Learning Language Through Firsthand Experiences

1.

2.

3.

4.

WORKSHOP

Facilitating Conversations

☐ Handout 3L15,
   pp. 65–66
☐ Handout 4E, p. 67
☐ Variations–Props,
   pictures

◖ PREPARATION

Duplicate the handouts.

◖ INTRODUCTION

Introduce the workshop:

- Research on early language development reveals that conversations matter. Talking with children provides them with experiences that are important to both their cognitive and their social/emotional learning (*Meaningful Differences*, Hart and Risely, 1995).

- In addition, the amount and frequency of language experiences matter. The more a child hears one or another aspect of the language, the greater the opportunity the child has to learn it.

- In *The Social World of Children Learning to Talk*, Betty Hart and Todd Risely (1999) conclude that the language tools provided to children through conversation can contribute at least as much to a child's future success as their heredity and their choice of friends.

- Given these powerful research findings, there is no question about the role conversations should play in the preschool classroom.

Lead a discussion about these ideas:

- Learning to take part in conversations is a complex process.

- Some say it is much like playing a game of basketball.

Ask:

- How is participating in a conversation like playing basketball?

     Possible responses:

     There are rules to follow.

     It takes two or more to play.

     It's a team effort; you have to work together to keep the game/conversation going.

A Trainer's Guide to The Creative Curriculum® for Preschool

You toss language/ball back and forth.

You have to know when and how to enter the game/conversation.

You must pay attention (i.e., look and listen) to know when to catch, pass, or shoot the language/ball.

Sometimes there are fouls or we step out of bounds.

There are ball/conversation "hogs."

Some players are more naturally skilled while others need more coaching.

Make the following points:

- Like novice basketball players, children are inexperienced conversationalists. The only way for them to learn the rules of conversation is to "play" or participate with someone who is more experienced.

- Once children learn the rules, they are better able to participate in conversations more readily and their capacity for language learning increases.

- As teachers, you are the experienced conversation players. Your role is to create opportunities for children to engage in conversations, help them learn the rules, and teach them how to "stay in the game."

◀ ACTIVITY

Introduce the activity:

- In a *Creative Curriculum* classroom, conversations occur frequently throughout the day. Some are formal or planned while others are spontaneous and informal.

- Some children and adults are skilled at carrying on conversations while others find it difficult and challenging.

- In this activity you will identify ways of engaging children in conversation for the purpose of promoting language and overall development.

Refer participants to handout 3L15 and give the following instructions:

- Read the scenario.

- Identify the strategies the teacher used to engage children in conversation and promote development. Record your ideas in column three.

Invite the participants to share their ideas.

> **Possible responses:** *Ms. Tory*
>
> *spoke with the children at their eye level*
>
> *built on the children's interests*
>
> *waited and recognized Tasheen's smile as a way of communicating*
>
> *matched the children's language abilities, i.e., she asked questions she knew they could answer*
>
> *used open-ended questions and comments to keep the conversation going*
>
> *added information or made relevant comments to indicate that she was listening.*

Distribute handout 4E. Then give the following instructions:

- In this activity, you will work with a partner or in teams of three. One of you will assume the role of a teacher and the other(s) the role of a child described in the scenario.

- As the teacher, you are to practice following the child's lead and teach conversational skills by modeling active listening (e.g., smile, make eye contact, or offer a related comment), asking relevant open-ended or clarifying questions to keep the conversation going, and demonstrating turn-taking skills.

- After you are finished, choose another scenario and switch roles until each of you has had a turn to play the role of the teacher.

Invite participants to react to the experience. Pose the following questions:

- What was most challenging for you?

- What does it mean to follow a child's lead? What is required?

- What messages do we send children when we engage them in genuine conversations?

SUMMARY

Summarize the workshop:

- Conversation contributes significantly to children's early language learning.

- By following the child's lead, that is, engaging in conversations about a topic the child chooses or building on the child's interests, teachers can help every child develop the language skills they need. And, they can create environments that encourage children to want to communicate.

◀ VARIATIONS

Variation 1:
Gather simple props from each interest area. Put enough props at each table so each pair of participants will have at least one.

Have participants form pairs. One will assume the role of a child and play with a prop. The other will assume the role of a teacher.

Explain that the teacher's role is to practice following the child's lead and teach conversational skills by modeling active listening (e.g., smile, make eye contact, or offer a related comment), asking relevant open-ended or clarifying questions to keep the conversation going, and demonstrating turn-taking skills.

Have participants switch roles using a different prop.

Variation 2:
Have participants form groups of 5. Put simple play props at each table.

Ask one person to assume the role of the teacher and the others to assume the role of one of the following types of children:

1. A child who initiates conversations and interactions and readily responds to others.
2. A child who rarely initiates conversations or interactions but responds when approached.
3. A child who initiates interactions or conversations when there is a need but otherwise is content to play alone.
4. A child who seldom initiates interactions or responds to others.

Explain that they are to pretend it is choice time and assume their role as the teacher tries to engage them in conversation and encourage interaction among others in the group.

Variation 3:
Have participants partner or form small groups of 3 or 4.

Have them read the activity, "Picture This" in *Literacy: The Creative Curriculum Approach*.

Give each group a collection of pictures. Ask them to take turns leading an informal discussion about a picture. Prior to leading the group each "teacher" should think about new words to introduce as well as open-ended questions to ask that would prompt or extend language and encourage conversation.

Variation 4:
Have participants form small groups of 3 or 4.

Have each person choose one thing they would like to share with the rest of the group. It may be a special keepsake from their purse or pocket, something they wish to teach the group, or some news they would like to share with the group such as the announcement of a new baby or grandchild.

Ask them to take turns assuming the role of the teacher while the others assume the role of children. The goal of the activity is to practice ways in which we can foster children language and conversational skills in group settings. In the role of teacher, the participant will want to model appropriate speaking and listening skills, prompt conversation by asking open-ended questions and encouraging others to ask questions, expanding on others comments, or rephrasing what someone has said.

Facilitating Conversation

The children in Ms. Tory's and Mr. Alvarez's preschool class arrive at varied times. They routinely put their things away, check to see if they have a job for the day, then work in interest areas until it is time for the morning meeting. Ms. Tory and Mr. Alvarez freely move about the room, greeting children and family members and interacting with the children.

Comments:

(Derek and Dallas enter the classroom, talking and laughing. They head toward the cubby area to hang up their jackets and backpacks.)

Dallas: *Not again, Derek!* (Laughs.) *That's my cubby. Here's yours.* (Points to Derek's cubby.)

Ms. Tory: (Stoops down and smiles at Derek.) *I think Dallas is right. Your name does have a capital* D, *like Dallas's name, see?* (Points to the Ds in both names.) *But your name is spelled capital* D-e-r-e-k, *and Dallas is spelled capital* D-a-l-l-a-s. (Points to each letter.) *Also remember that your picture is here to help you and to let others know that this is your cubby.*

Ms. Tory: (Smiles at Tasheen, who reluctantly enters the classroom with her dad, and stoops to speak to Tasheen as she unpacks her backpack.) *Welcome back. We missed having you at school these past few days. We have lots to share with you, and I bet you have lots to share with us.*

Tasheen: (Smiles at Ms. Tory but doesn't speak.)

Ms. Tory: *I heard that you are now a big sister. Your mom and dad are so lucky to have you to help them with the new baby!*

From *Literacy: The Creative Curriculum® Approach*
©2005 Teaching Strategies, Inc., PO Box 42243, Washington, DC 20015; www.TeachingStrategies.com

Facilitating Conversation, continued

Tasheen:	(Takes a picture from her backpack and shows it to Ms. Tory.)
Ms. Tory:	*Ahhh, I see you brought a picture of you and the new baby to share with your friends. What are you going to tell your friends about the new baby?*

Tasheen:	*It's a boy, and his name is Jeremiah.*
Ms. Tory:	*He looks like he's smiling. Is he a happy baby?*
Tasheen:	*Sometimes he cries a lot, and it is really loud.*
Ms. Tory:	*Babies do cry a lot sometimes. I wonder why.*
Tasheen:	*Dad said they can't talk, so they cry to let us know they need something.* (Tasheen and Dad smile at one another.) *Sometimes he cries because he's hungry or when he needs his diaper changed. Sometimes he just wants us to hold him.*
Ms. Tory:	*He's not crying here. He must like it when you hold him like that.* (Points to the picture, and Tasheen smiles.)
	I know you have lots more to tell your friends about Jeremiah. What do you need to do in order to share your picture?
Tasheen:	*Put it in the Share Chair.* (Ms. Tory nods; Tasheen hugs her Dad goodbye and skips off with her picture.)

Responding to Children—Scenarios

 A

Leo and Kate are busy in the Block Area putting a ramp in various positions to form an incline to roll vehicles down. You've noticed that they have tried leaning the ramp against the wall, on the shelf, and against a chair.

 B

Carlos is in the Dramatic Play Area where he puts on a cape and announces that he is Batman. He proceeds to climb on a nearby chair and jump off.

 C

Susie takes a milkweed leaf that had been collected on a nature walk from the Discovery Area and places it under the computer microscope. With great excitement she exclaims, "Those white things are bugs!"

 D

Shawn is in the Toys and Games area diligently putting together puzzle-like dominos. On one end of each domino is a numeral and on the other end is a set of objects. After she matches the pieces, she lays the domino in its original box, focusing on keeping the matched pieces together.

 E

Janelle is at the easel painting pictures of swirling colors. You hear her making whirring sounds and she says, "You better watch out. Oh no, here comes a tornado!"

 F

Ben spends the entire outdoor time in the sandbox repeatedly filling cups with sand and pouring them into a bucket. Then he takes the bucket and dumps it in another area.

 G

Tasheen spends most of her time on the playground playing "monster" and trying to scare the other children.

 H

Dallas and Zack carefully examine the shells in the Toys and Games Area. They put the shells into two piles, then three, and then four.

©2004 Teaching Strategies, Inc., PO Box 42243, Washington, DC 20015, www.TeachingStrategies.com **4E**

WORKSHOP

Using Songs, Rhymes, and Other Language Play Activities

☐ Bumble bee puppet
☐ Materials for small-group work based on selected activities from *Literacy*, Chapter 5

PREPARATION

Gather or prepare the materials to be used in the selected small-group activities.

INTRODUCTION

Introduce the workshop:

- Songs, rhymes, and fingerplays are typically a part of the preschool program day.

- Their content often reflects people, animals, or objects children can easily identify with, and children enjoy the repeated and rhythmic language patterns.

- In this activity, you will explore ways in which songs, rhymes, and other language games can be used to address the components of literacy in an intentional way.

Use one or more songs, rhymes, and language games to demonstrate how the components of literacy can be addressed. Suggestions follow. Note however that suggestions three and four are not meant to be used with children; they illustrate how literacy instruction can be playful.

1. Use a hand puppet, preferably a bumble bee puppet to demonstrate the rhyme *Bippity, Boppity Bumble Bee*. Invite participants to join you.

   Bippity, boppity, bumble bee,
   Can you say your name for me?
   (Point to a participant to say his name).
   Repeat the name.

   Let's all clap it (clap once for each syllable).
   Let's all snap it (snap once for each syllable).
   Let's all stamp it (stamp once for each syllable).

   Invite participants to suggest other ways to say the syllables in someone's name (e.g., tap, blink, or march). **Component: Phonological Awareness (syllable awareness, rhyme, alliteration)**

2. Invite participants to join you in reciting a familiar nursery rhyme (e.g., *Little Miss Muffet*) or singing a familiar song (e.g., *The Itsy, Bitsy Spider*). Have them identify any words that may be unfamiliar to children and describe ways in which they would help children understand their meanings (See the activity titled *All Kinds of Spiders*). **Component: Vocabulary and Language**

3. Invite participants to sing *My Bonnie Lies Over the Ocean*. Sing the song a second time, but tell participants to listen for the words that begin with the /b/ sound. Each time they hear the sound they will stand or sit alternately.

> *My Bonnie* (stand) *lies over the ocean.*
> *My Bonnie* (sit) *lies over the sea.*
> *My Bonnie* (stand) *lies over the ocean.*
> *Oh, bring* (sit) *back* (stand) *my Bonnie* (sit) *to me.*
>
> *Bring back*
> *Bring back*
> *Oh, bring back my Bonnie to me, to me*
> *Bring back*
> *Bring back*
> *Oh, bring back my Bonnie to me.*

Component: Phonological Awareness (alliteration)

4. Invite participants to try this alliterative activity. Give these instructions:

- Introduce yourself to others at your table. Tell them something about you by using words that begin with the same sound as the sound at the beginning of your name (e.g., My name is Cooking Candy. I constantly crave cake, candies, and other confections.)

Point out that tongue twisters are especially useful in helping children to attend to the beginning sounds of words. **Component: Phonological Awareness (alliteration)**

Make the following points:

- Singing, reciting rhymes and tongue twisters, and playing language games are enjoyable for children and should be used daily.

- Beyond singing and reciting these for enjoyment, teachers can use them to intentionally:

  promote children's listening skills

  draw attention to the sounds of language (rhyme, alliteration, syllables)

  teach new vocabulary

  help children learn about the structure of language

  promote children's knowledge and understanding of print

◀ ACTIVITY

Assign each table of participants one or more of the following activities found in Chapter 5 of *Literacy: The Creative Curriculum Approach*. Provide the necessary materials associated with each activity.

- All Kinds of Spiders
- Did You Ever See?
- Clap a Friend's Name
- Friends
- Give the Dog a Bone
- I Spy with My Little Eye
- Me Too
- Who Ate the Cookies?
- Poetry in Motion
- Rhyme Time
- Rhyming Riddles
- Rhyming Tubs
- Who Will Jump the Candlestick?

Have them read the activity assigned to their group and prepare to demonstrate it.

Explain that they should identify the component(s) of literacy addressed by the activity, identify the setting(s) most appropriate for the activity (large- or small-group time, transition, outdoors, etc.), and discuss any additional ideas or adaptations they might make to the activity.

Invite each group to present.

◀ SUMMARY

Summarize the workshop:

- Children enjoy singing songs, reciting rhymes and tongue twisters, and playing other language games.

- And, the rhyme and rhythmic language patterns encourage children to further explore language on their own, making these playful activities powerful teaching and learning tools.

NOTES

Reading Aloud

WORKSHOPS

 Key Points	 Workshop	 Materials	Time (minutes)
Reading to and with children every day encourages a love of books and reading.	**Motivating Young Children to Read** (p. 74)	☐ *The Wednesday Surprise* by Eve Bunting ☐ Handout 3L16: Reflections on Reading ☐ *Literacy,* pp. 9–10	20
Reading aloud to children helps them learn important skills and concepts.	**Selecting Books to Read Aloud** (p. 78)	☐ Collections of books ☐ Handout 3L17: Selecting Books for Reading Aloud and the Library Area ☐ Transparency 3L18: Reading Various Types of Books . . . ☐ *Literacy,* p. 81, Appendix	15
Interactive reading has a very positive effect on children's literacy learning.	**Reading Aloud** (p. 82)	☐ Book collections ☐ *Silly Sally* by Audrey Wood or another big book ☐ Prop for read aloud demonstration ☐ Handout 3L19: Interactive Reading Model ☐ Handout 3L20: Planning for Reading Aloud ☐ Variation–Handout 3L21: Read Aloud Scenario ☐ *Literacy,* pp. 58–65, 83–85, 140–141, 198, 202, 216, 230, Appendix ☐ Materials for selected reading activities	30
Teachers need to purposefully interact with children during reading experiences.	**Responding to Children as Readers** (p. 94)	☐ Handout 10E: Skills for Engaging With Books ☐ *Creative Curriculum* video ☐ *Literacy,* pp. 136–137, 139–141, Appendix	30–40
Children's literacy learning increases when families and teachers work as partners.	**Involving Families in Children's Literacy Learning** (p. 100)	☐ Handout 3L22: Involving Families in Children's Literacy Learning ☐ Collections of books ☐ *Literacy,* p. 90	60

Motivating Young Children to Read

☐ *The Wednesday Surprise*
☐ Handout 3L16, p. 77
☐ *Literacy*, pp. 9–10

PREPARATION

Become familiar with the book *The Wednesday Surprise* by Eve Bunting.

Duplicate the handout.

INTRODUCTION

Introduce the workshop by reading the book *The Wednesday Surprise* by Eve Bunting to participants.

Ask participants to identify factors that contributed to Grandma's ability to learn to read. List them on chart paper.

> **Possible responses:**
>
> *Grandma was motivated. She had a desire to learn to read.*
>
> *Others encouraged her.*
>
> *There was sufficient time and opportunity for learning.*
>
> *The environment was free of risks.*
>
> *Reading was a shared experience. Grandma learned to read by reading with a more skilled reader.*
>
> *There was a regularly scheduled time for reading (every Wednesday night). Anna and Grandma were committed to one another.*
>
> *Anna was a willing teacher who offered support and enthusiasm for Grandma's efforts.*
>
> *Grandma practiced regularly.*

Use the items listed as a means of drawing parallels to classroom practice. Ask:

- What does this imply for your classroom practice?

- How can you set the stage for children to learn to read?

Summarize the discussion with the following points:

- Most of you probably remember times when a parent, other family member, teacher, or another adult read aloud to you.

- These reading experiences more than likely influenced how you feel about reading today.

- The purpose of this workshop is to identify factors that make reading aloud a powerful strategy for motivating children to read and promoting children's literacy learning.

◀ ACTIVITY

Distribute the handout and give the following instructions:

- Complete the questions on your own.

- When you are finished, turn to the person next to you and share your experience.

Invite participants to share ideas from their discussions with the whole group.

Make the following points:

- Reading is a relaxing pastime for most of us. It provides an opportunity to learn new things, escape to other places, and explore new worlds.

- As you reflected on your childhood, you may have recalled titles of favorite books, remembered special times when you and family members, friends, or teachers shared books, or perhaps recalled a creative experience you had in connection with a particular story.

- These types of experiences may have motivated you to continue reading, since reading habits and motivation to read often develop early in life.

- Research indicates that reading to children at school or at home leads them to associate reading with pleasure and provides them with models of reading (Morrow, 2001).

Lead a discussion about what teachers can do to make children's literacy experiences positive. Use the points in "What is the Teacher's Role in Literacy as a Source of Enjoyment?" on pages 9–10 in *Literacy: The Creative Curriculum Approach* as a framework for your discussion.

◀ SUMMARY

Summarize the workshop:

- Motivation plays a key role in children's ability to learn to read.

- When you share books with young children daily, you help to instill a love for books and reading, thereby motivating children to want to learn to read.

- In a *Creative Curriculum* classroom, teachers read aloud to children at least twice daily. And, they make a point to share books with individual or small groups of children during Choice Time.

NOTES

Reflections on Reading

1. What do you remember about reading as a child?

2. What was your favorite book when you were a child? Why?

3. Do you enjoy reading as an adult? Why or why not?

4. How have your own experiences affected your classroom practice?

3L16

WORKSHOP

Selecting Books to Read Aloud

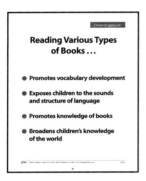

☐ Handout 3L17, p. 80
☐ Transparency 3L18, p. 81
☐ *Literacy*, p. 81, Appendix

◀ PREPARATION

Duplicate the handout. Prepare enough copies so each participant can review two to three books.

Prepare the transparency.

Put a collection of books at each table of participants. The collection should include books from a variety of genres (e.g., informational/nonfiction; folktales; fairy tales; concept: vehicles, counting, signs, alphabet, colors; picture storybooks; wordless; predictable; nursery rhymes; songbooks; poetry). Include books that show children with disabilities, children of color, as well as the typical interests of the children with whom the teachers work. You may ask each teacher to bring one or two books from their classroom collections or have the program sponsor provide the books.

◀ INTRODUCTION

Introduce the workshop:

* Reading aloud not only motivates young children to read, it is an effective way to teach skills and concepts about reading.

* The information in books builds children's background knowledge. Through books, children are introduced to new and varied people, places, ideas, and concepts. This knowledge contributes to children's ability to comprehend what they will read later.

* When children watch and listen to teachers reading books aloud, they learn many important literacy skills and concepts they will need when learning to read and write independently.

* In this workshop, you will review various types (genre) of books and consider how they contribute to children's learning, in particular, their literacy learning.

◀ ACTIVITY

Explain that each person will examine two to three books to determine if they are suitable for reading aloud.

Refer participants to the chart on page 81 of *Literacy: The Creative Curriculum Approach* and review the section, "Characteristics of a Good Book to Read Aloud."

Distribute the handout. Have participants answer the questions as they review each book.

Have participants share at their tables a favorite book they reviewed and discuss how they would use it to support children's literacy learning.

Refer participants to the Literacy Implementation Checklist in the Appendix. Review

- Item 2, Literacy in the Overall Environment. This item addresses the quality of books and states that children need access to 3 or more books from **each** of the following categories: narrative, predictable, alphabet, number/counting, informational, and rhyming books. **These books can be in any interest area in the classroom.**

- Item 6, Literacy in the Library Area: Display (with covers facing out) at least 25 children's books (e.g., storybooks; nursery rhymes; and informational, predictable, alphabet, and number/counting books).

SUMMARY

Use the transparency and share examples of favorite books as you discuss each point:

- In a *Creative Curriculum* classroom, teachers read books that relate to the children's culture, interests, and life experiences as well as books that help children develop understandings about the world. And, teachers intentionally select books to address the goals they have for children's learning.

- Books from all genre (types or categories) are shared including informational/nonfiction books, folktales, fairy tales, concept books, picture storybooks, wordless books, predictable books, nursery rhymes, songbooks, poetry, and alphabet books.

- Reading various types of books:

    Promotes vocabulary development. Children hear new and rare words and they learn new expressions.

    Exposes children to the sounds and structure of language. Children hear and attend to the similarities and differences in the sounds of words. They hear the language of books, language that is more formal and sophisticated than conversational language.

    Promotes children's knowledge of books. They learn about the characteristics and structure of different kinds of stories and learn that there are multiple ways in which to communicate thoughts, ideas, and information. They learn the routines, skills, and language used in reading and sharing books.

    Broadens children's knowledge of the world by introducing them to new and varied people, places, ideas, and concepts. This knowledge contributes to their ability to comprehend what they read.

Selecting Books for Reading Aloud and the Library Area

Choose one book to read and then answer the questions below.

Title of Book: _____

Author: _____

1. What would children like about this book?

2. Is this book more appropriate for younger preschoolers or older preschoolers? Why?

3. What could children learn through this book?

4. How are children's language and literacy skills promoted through this book?

5. Does this book reflect diversity and/or promote inclusion? If yes, how?

6. Would you include this book in your Library Area? Why or why not?

Reading Various Types of Books . . .

● **Promotes vocabulary development**

● **Exposes children to the sounds and structure of language**

● **Promotes knowledge of books**

● **Broadens children's knowledge of the world**

WORKSHOP

Reading Aloud

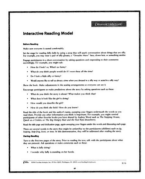

☐ Handout 3L19,
   pp. 87–88
☐ Handout 3L20, p. 89
☐ Handout 3L21,
   pp. 90–93
☐ *Literacy*, pp. 58–65,
   83–85, 140–141, 198,
   202, 216, 230, Appendix
☐ Book collections
☐ *Silly Sally* or another
   big book
☐ Prop for read-aloud
   demonstration
☐ Materials for selected
   reading activities

PREPARATION

Duplicate the handout.

In this workshop, you will model interactive story reading for the purpose of demonstrating how reading aloud is appropriately and intentionally used as a teaching tool. A description of an interactive reading demonstration using the big book version of *Silly Sally* by Audrey Wood is included for you as handout 3L19, Interactive Reading Model. The use of this model is optional and the strategies, questions, and statements described are suggestions and should be expanded upon based on your situation. Any book can be used by following the guidelines described on pages 83–85 and pages 140–141 of *Literacy: The Creative Curriculum Approach*.

Prior to the workshop, ask a small group of participants to volunteer to pretend they are young children listening to a story. Later in the workshop you will ask them sit on the floor or in chairs, wherever they are most comfortable to act out their roles.

Put a collection of books on each table or have participants bring a favorite book reviewed in the previous workshop.

Become familiar with the literacy activities referenced in this workshop.

INTRODUCTION

Ask:

* When do you read to your children? How often?

   Possible responses:

   large- and small-group times

   individually in the Library Area

   outdoors

   during snack time

   after outdoor play

   before rest time

   prior to departure for the day

- How do they know it is story time? In what ways do you make it special?

    Possible responses:

    I wear a special hat or apron.

    I play music or recite a chant or fingerplay.

    There is a special area designated just for story time.

Explain that in a *Creative Curriculum* classroom, teachers read aloud to children at least twice a day.

Make the following points:

- Teachers establish regular times to read aloud, such as the beginning and end of the day; and, they look for opportunities to share books at other times in small-group settings, individually with children in the Library and other interest areas, as well as with the whole class.

- Teachers create special places for reading where children can sit comfortably and be near enough to hear the teacher and see the pictures clearly. Whether it is the Library Area or another space, children come to recognize the area as a special place for sharing books with friends.

- Most often, the first reading of a story is for enjoyment and for children to hear the flow of the story. When children hear stories they enjoy, they are likely to ask you to read them again, and again.

- Research indicates that it is the way in which a teacher reads that has a significant impact on children's language and literacy learning.

- During this workshop, you will explore reading strategies that intentionally promote the development of literacy skills and concepts.

ACTIVITY

Invite the volunteers to come forward.

Explain to the remaining participants that the volunteers have agreed to assume the roles of children for the purpose of demonstrating an effective interactive story time.

Have the remaining participants observe your behaviors and interactions with the volunteers and jot down the strategies you use.

Read *Silly Sally* or another big book to the volunteer group using interactive reading techniques.

After the demonstration, thank the volunteers and have them return to their tables.

Have participants discuss at their tables, the techniques you used and which components of literacy were addressed. Invite them to share their ideas with the whole group.

Refer participants to the section titled "Effective Ways to Read Aloud" on pages 83–85 and to "Interactive Story Reading" on pages 140–141 in *Literacy The Creative Curriculum Approach* as you summarize the discussion.

Distribute handout 3L19 if you wish.

Call attention to the adaptations and accommodations for reading aloud to children who are advanced, have disabilities, or are English language learners found on pages 58–65 in *Literacy: The Creative Curriculum Approach*.

Lead a discussion about the importance of planning for read aloud.

Refer participants to handout 3L20 and the collection of books on their tables. Have them choose a book and complete the handout.

Next, have them choose a partner and read their stories to one another using the ideas recorded on their handout.

Invite participants to share their thoughts about the experience. Explain that this form is meant to be used as a framework while they are learning to conduct interactive story reading.

Refer participants to the Literacy Implementation Checklist in the Appendix of *Literacy: The Creative Curriculum Approach*. Review items 1, 3, 4, and 5. Have participants assess themselves on these items.

Make the following points:

- On occasion, you will want to use stories for the express purpose of addressing a specific literacy skill.

- Some model storybook activities have been provided for you in chapter 5 of *Literacy: The Creative Curriculum Approach*.

Lead the following activities or have participants form groups to demonstrate each.

- Be a Word, p. 198
- Can You Do It?, p. 202
- Feed Me, p. 216
- Listen for the Word, p. 230

Invite participants to brainstorm ways the same strategies could be used with different texts.

SUMMARY

Summarize the workshop:

- Children's language development and comprehension are positively influenced when adults involve them in the story by asking open-ended questions, adding information, and prompting them to make a connection to their prior experiences.

- Children's knowledge of print concepts is enhanced through direct contact with books and explicit modeling by skilled readers.

- While sharing books with the whole class is an appropriate activity, the type of interaction we have been discussing is not encouraged because the flow of the story is interrupted with so many children participating.

- During small-group and one-on-one reading experiences, children interact more, generate more questions and comments, and therefore develop comprehension skills. For this reason, it is important that teachers read regularly to children in small groups and individually.

VARIATION

Distribute handout 3L21.

Have participants read the scenario and then record the strategies Ms. Tory used to make story time effective.

Have participants work in pairs or as a small group to compare and discuss their responses.

Debrief their discussions.

Have participants select a book and plan a read aloud using handout 3L20, Planning for Reading Aloud.

Have participants choose a partner and read their books to one another.

Lead the following activities or have participants form groups to demonstrate each of the following activities described in Chapter 5 of *Literacy: The Creative Curriculum Approach*.

- Listen for the Word
- Be a Word
- Feed Me
- Can You Do It?

Invite participants to brainstorm ways the same strategies could be used with different texts.

NOTES

Interactive Reading Model

Before Reading

Make sure everyone is seated comfortably.

Set the stage for reading *Silly Sally* by using a prop that will spark conversation about things that are silly. For example, you may wear a pair of silly glasses, a "Groucho Marx" face, clown hair, or something similar.

Engage participants in a short conversation by asking questions and responding to their comments accordingly. For example, you might ask:

- How do I look? or, What's so funny?

- What do you think people would do if I wore these all the time?

- Do I look a little silly or funny?

- Would anyone like to tell us about a time when you dressed in a silly way or acted in a silly way?

Show the book. Make adjustments in the seating arrangements so everyone can see it.

Encourage participants to make predictions about the story by asking questions such as these:

- What do you think the story is about? What makes you think that?

- What does it look like the girl is doing?

- How would you describe the girl?

- How do you think she feels? How do you know?

Read the title of the book and the author's name, sweeping your fingers underneath the words as you read them. Provide any other information you think is important. For example, you might remind participants of other favorite books you have shared by Audrey Wood and Don Wood such as *The Napping House*, *Quick as a Cricket*, or *The Little Mouse, the Red Ripe Strawberry, and the Big Hungry Bear*.

Read the title page and dedication page, again sweeping your fingers under the words and discussing each page.

There are several words in the story that might be unfamiliar to the participants (children) such as *jig*, *leaping*, *leap-frog*, *loon*, or *tune*. In this demonstration, they will be addressed after reading the story.

During Reading

Turn to the first two pages of the story. Prior to reading the text, talk with the participants about what they see pictured. Ask questions or make comments such as these:

- What is Sally doing?

- I wonder why Sally is standing on her hands.

- Where do you think Sally is going? I wonder how she will get there.

Interactive Reading Model, continued

- I wonder who she will meet along the way. What do you think? Is there anything in the picture that might give you a clue?

- Who do you think Sally will meet first? Why? Second? Third? Fourth?

Read the story; but, before reading the text on each page, ask participants to make predictions about what it might say. Have them confirm their predictions or note when they were incorrect. Occasionally leave off a word at the end of a sentence and ask participants fill it in. Ask questions and make comments that encourage reasoning and help children make connections to the story:

- What do you think would happen if everyone walked upside down on their hands?

- How do you think you would feel if you walked upside down all of the time?

- I wonder if pigs can really dance. Have you ever seen a pig dance?

- Have you ever played leap frog?

- What do think Sally will do when she meets the sheep? Can you think of a word that rhymes with sheep?

- Sally and her friends are sleeping. Have you ever seen anyone sleep upside down?

- I wonder if Sally and her friends will ever make it to town?

After Reading
Ask questions such as these to encourage participants to respond to the story or recall certain story elements:

- What did you like best about this story? or What did you think was the silliest part of the story?

- On the way to town, Sally met a loon who sang a ___ (tune). Who can tell me what a loon is? Can you think of another word for tune?

- Who knows or can show us how to play leap frog?

- What do you notice about the words Silly and Sally?

- Would you say this story was real or make believe? Why?

If time permits, extend the story by inviting participants to name some different characters Sally might meet on her next trip to town. Record their ideas on chart paper. Ask if participants would like to write a book about the silly characters they suggested.

Dismiss the participants one at a time using a favorite transition activity. For example, you might say, "Laughing Linda, you may leap to your table."

Planning for Reading Aloud

Title of Book: _____

Author: _____

Addressing the Components of Literacy
List the component(s) of literacy that are addressed with this book.

Before Reading
Describe your plans for introducing the book. List aspects of the book (e.g., author, illustrator, characters, setting, or type of book) you will discuss, open-ended questions you might ask prior to reading, props, or other strategies (e.g., sing a song related to the story topic) you might use to pique children's interest in the book. List new vocabulary words you plan to introduce.

During Reading
Develop at least three open-ended questions/comments you could use during reading to help children comprehend the text. Describe your plans for accommodating the needs of the English language learner or a child with a disability (e.g., use gestures or props to clarify words, paraphrase text).

After Reading
Develop questions/comments you could use to encourage children to respond to certain story elements (e.g., "I wonder why the fox....., How was the story of _Chicken Little_ similar to _Henny Penny?_") Describe any plans for extending the story (e.g., having children respond to the story through drawing or writing).

Reading Aloud Scenario

It is choice time, and the children are engaged in various activities throughout the room. Ms. Tory picks up the xylophone and begins to play a soft melody. Looking up from their play, the children see Ms. Tory making her way toward the rocking chair in the Library Area. The children begin putting away their materials, then eagerly join Ms. Tory, one by one, as she sits holding a large round gold box in her lap. Mr. Alvarez helps children who are still cleaning up and then they too, join the other children on the rug. Ms. Tory makes sure everyone is comfortable and comments on how well the children cleaned up. Mr. Alvarez joins the group, and Ms. Tory begins story time.

Comments:

Ms. Tory:	*Today I have a story for you about a girl who gets a gift that disappoints her a little. Does anyone know what I mean by disappointed?*
Dallas:	*Sad.*
Setsuko:	*Yeah, sad because you think you're going to get something and then you don't get it.*
Ms. Tory:	*Have you ever been disappointed?* (Children offer examples of disappointments.) *Show me how your face looks when you are disappointed.*
Ms. Tory:	*The gift the girl was waiting for was something you wear on your head. Can anyone guess what that might be?*
Various children:	*A scarf! A cap! A hat! A visor! A football helmet!*
Ms. Tory:	*Those are all ideas of things someone might wear on his or her head. Why would someone need or want to wear something on her head?*
Sonya:	*My grandma wears a scarf on her head so her hair won't blow everywhere.*
Leo:	*My Dad wears a cap to keep the sun out of his eyes.*
Crystal:	*Yeah, My Mom wears a visor to keep the sun out, too.*

Reading Aloud Scenario, continued

Dallas:	*And football players wear helmets so their heads won't get hurt when they get tackled! You have to wear a helmet if you play football. It's a rule!*
Ms. Tory:	*Those things help to protect us—from sun, getting hurt, or getting our hair all messed up.*

Ms. Tory holds up the box and asks the children to think to themselves about which of the items they mentioned is most likely to be in the box. She asks them to listen while she gently shakes the box.

Ms. Tory:	*Do you think this could be a football helmet?*
Setsuko:	*No. The box isn't big enough.*
Dallas:	*And we would hear a clunking sound.*
Ms. Tory:	*How about a scarf?*
Sonya:	*No. A scarf doesn't need a box. My grandma keeps her scarves folded in a drawer in her dresser.*

Ms. Tory slowly cracks open the lid of the box to reveal a small section of the brim of a straw hat.

Leo:	*I think it's a cap, because I saw that piece that hangs over your face.*
Ms. Tory:	*You mean you saw the brim? A cap does have a brim, but so do a visor and a hat. Let's take a look at what's in the box.*
	(Ms. Tory takes the hat out of the box, briefly talks about it, then places it on top of her head.) *It's not a football helmet, a scarf, or a cap. But, it does have a brim, as Leo thought.*

Comments:

Ms. Tory: *The title of this story is* Jennie's Hat, *and the author's name is Ezra Jack Keats.* (Ms. Tory holds up the book and runs her fingers underneath the words as she reads.)

(She points to the cover picture of the girl with the basket on her head and leads a discussion about who the girl might be and why she has a basket on her head.)

(She shows the first several pages of the story and asks the children to describe what they see and predict what they think will happen.)

(She returns to the beginning of the book and reads the first few pages about Jennie's disappointment in her new hat.)

Tyrone: *She didn't like her hat!*

Ms. Tory: *Jennie was disappointed in her hat. Have you ever cried because you were disappointed?*

Ms. Tory: (Continues to read.) *"She put on a straw basket to see what sort of hat it would make. Then she drew pictures. 'HAT-CHOO!,' she sneezed. 'Bless you, dear,' called her mother, 'and what are you doing?' 'I'm drawing a hat-erpillar—I mean a caterpillar,' answered Jennie.'"*

Have you ever heard anyone sneeze like that? (Children shake their heads, no.) *What do you think a hat-erpillar is?*

Dallas: (Children sit quietly. Then Dallas points to the picture on the page and responds.) *Not a hat-erpillar, a caterpillar! See, there is the picture of the caterpillar!*

Ms. Tory: *Why do you think Jennie called it a hat-erpillar?* (Children offer a variety of responses. Ms. Tory continues reading and asking questions.)

Reading Aloud Scenario, continued

Ms. Tory: (Continues reading.)

Carlos: *The birds are following Jennie.*

Ms. Tory: *Hmm, I wonder why?* (Pauses.)

Ms. Tory: (Reads text about the birds that swooped down, flapping and fluttering around Jennie's new hat. She makes swooping movements with her arms and flaps her hands as she does so. Ms. Tory invites the children to join her making flapping, fluttering, and swooping motions.)

Why were the birds following Jennie?

Children: *To put things on her hat!*

Crystal: *Jennie is happy now! But she wasn't at first, when she just had that plain hat.*

Dallas: *The birds were Jennie's friends.*

Setsuko: *Jennie's hat is beautiful now!*

Ms. Tory: (Finishes the story.) *And that's the end of the story.*

Sonya: *Why did her mom wrap up her hat?*

Ms. Tory: *Well, what did the story say?* (Ms. Tory points to the last sentence and reads it again.) *"It would be saved and looked at and remembered for a long, long time."*

Did you enjoy the story? What did you like best?

I'll put Jennie's Hat *in the Library Area, along with this hat.* (Takes the hat off of her head.) *You may read it on your own or with a friend.*

Responding to Children as Readers

□ Handout 10E,
   pp. 98–99
□ *Creative Curriculum*
   video
□ *Literacy,* pp. 136–137,
   139–141, Appendix

◖ PREPARATION

Duplicate the handout.

Cue the *Creative Curriculum* video to the Library segment.

Prior to the workshop, have participants observe one or two children in their class Library Area and record the reading behaviors they notice.

◖ INTRODUCTION

Introduce the workshop with the following question and have participants discuss it at their tables:

- When it comes to learning language (oral and written), how are children like scientists?

     Possible responses:

     Gather information (listen and observe others speaking, reading, and writing).

     Form hypotheses (construct rules about how language works).

     Explore, experiment, test, or try out their new information.

     Reach a conclusion, seek confirmation.

Make the following points:

- Language and literacy learning is a complex process that involves many skills. Like scientists, young children construct their understanding of how language works by observing and exploring.

- Left alone, most children don't become literate. They must have many opportunities to observe and interact with adults and others in meaningful situations in order to refine their understandings.

- Some children enter school with early reading skills, while others are being read to for the first time.

- If all children are to become literate, teachers must

     know the specific skills children need to learn to read

     observe children to find out what they know

     use what they learn about children to guide their literacy learning

- In a *Creative Curriculum* classroom, the Library Area is the hub of literacy learning. It's the primary place where children go to practice or make sense of what they experienced during story time and other literacy experiences.

- There is a direct relationship between your literacy behavior and children's behavior in the Library Area. Enjoyable, interactive story times are likely to influence children to read books, model reading behaviors, and engage in other literacy experiences in the Library Area.

- During this workshop you will examine the skills and behaviors children acquire as they engage in the reading process and identify strategies that will support their progress.

ACTIVITY

Show the "Library Area" segment of the *Creative Curriculum* video. Have participants watch for ways in which the teachers become involved with children.

Briefly discuss the video. Then make some general points:

- It is easy to overlook children who are working in the Library Area and to focus attention on children in other more active, noisy interest areas.

- Much can be learned about children while they are in the Library Area. Teachers need to make time each day to visit the area to observe and interact with children.

- An appropriate starting point for your observations is to begin to look for reading behaviors children exhibit while engaged with books.

Have participants turn to pages 136–137 in *Literacy: The Creative Curriculum Approach* and read the section, "Skills for Engaging with Books." Provide clarifying information about each skill if necessary. Emphasize that these skills develop simultaneously rather than in a linear or sequential fashion.

Have participants review the observations from their classroom to determine which reading skills the children are demonstrating.

Next, distribute the handout. Have participants work in pairs to discuss each scenario and determine which skill(s) each best represents. Also have them look at the objectives under "Language" in the Appendix of *Literacy: The Creative Curriculum Approach* to identify any related objectives.

Still working in pairs, have participants determine what they could do or say to support or extend children's literacy learning.

Invite participants to share their responses.

Call attention to the strategies for reading with individual children outlined on pages 139–141 of *Literacy: The Creative Curriculum Approach*. Point out that reading with individual children and small groups of children are opportune times to focus on specific skills.

SUMMARY

Summarize the workshop:

*   Observing children in the Library Area provides you with a picture of each child's interests and skills in literacy-related activities.

*   With this information, you can plan how to respond to each child to promote learning.

NOTES

Skills for Engaging With Books

1. The teacher prepares to read the book, *The Grouchy Ladybug* by Eric Carle to a small group of children. Carlos points to the picture on the front of the book and says, "Look at that ladybug. I see lots of ladybugs around my house. Is this book going to be about a ladybug?"

2. Kate and Leo are in the Library Area retelling the story *I Know an Old Lady Who Swallowed a Fly* (Westcott) using a pocket puppet and props. Juwan enters the Library Area and says, "You're not telling it right. She swallows the dog first and then the cat." Kate insists that they are correct and tells Juwan to look in the book. Juwan turns the pages one at a time naming the fly, spider, bird, cat, and then the dog. He looks at Kate and Leo, smiles and says, "uh, oh."

3. At morning meeting, Mr. Alvarez holds up a big book and says, "I'm going to read a story called *Caps for Sale* (Esphyr Slobodkina). Sonya asks, "What are caps?" Mr. Alvarez points to a cap in the picture and says "A cap is a little hat that you wear on your head." Sonya replies, "I've worn a hat before, but not a cap." Derek says, "I wear a baseball cap, but it looks different than that one."

4. Alexa and Susie are in the Library Area during choice time. They chose to read and retell the story *It Looked Like Spilt Milk* (Charles Shaw) using felt pieces. Alexa decides that she will "read" while Susie puts the felt pieces on the board. Alexa opens the book to begin and Susie puts the first felt piece on the board. Alexa takes the piece down and says to Susie, "You have to wait until I read!" Alexa runs her fingers under the text in a sweeping motion, reciting the familiar words of the story. She looks at Susie and says, "Now you can put up the spilt milk piece."

5. While outdoors, Jonelle and Zack discover a variety of insects near a decaying tree stump. Jonelle hurries to get Mr. Alvarez and shows him their discovery. Remembering an earlier experience in using a book to identify birds nesting in a nearby tree, Zack asks Mr. Alvarez if he can get them a book that will tell them more about the bugs they found.

6. Tasheen asks Ms. Tory to read the story, *The Teeny-Tiny Woman* (Paul Galdone), to her in the Library Area. They sit together in the bean bag chair looking at the cover of the book. Tasheen says, "This book has my name in it." "See, here's a "T" and here's a "T" (she points to Teeny and Tiny). That's my name." Ms. Tory reads the title. Tasheen says, "See, I told you, teeny, tiny, and Tasheen. We all start the same."

10E

Skills for Engaging With Books, continued

7. Mr. Alvarez watches Setsuko and Crystal in the Discovery Area as they observe the tree frogs in the terrarium. He listens as the girls talk about how and why they think the frogs jump about so much. The girls move to the Library Area to find the book *Jump, Frog, Jump!* (Robert Kalan), a class favorite. They climb on the sofa and together they point at each word on the cover and recite in unison, *Jump, Frog, Jump.* They continue to retell the events of the story in their own words, but point to each word when they come to the repetitive phrase "jump, frog, jump."

8. Ben hurries to Ms. Tory with two books in his hands, *Mama, Do You Love Me?* (Barbara Joose) and *Is Your Mama a Llama?* (Steven Kellogg). He says, "Look Ms. Tory. I found two books about Big Mama. See it says Mama (points to the word Mama on each book). Note: Ben enjoys making cards and writing letters for his grandmother, "Big Mama," who lives with him. Ms. Tory has included "Big Mama" in Ben's collection of favorite words. He refers to it often when writing.

Involving Families in Children's Literacy Learning

☐ Handout 3L22, p. 103

◀ PREPARATION

Duplicate the handout.

Prepare a transparency of the handout.

Prior to the workshop, contact participants and ask them to bring one or two of their favorite children's books. Or, contact an organization that is willing to donate books to your class/school/center to create a family lending library.

◀ INTRODUCTION

Introduce the workshop:

- Just as you get to know each child and use what you learn to develop a relationship, you can build partnerships with families by getting to know and appreciate each family's unique characteristics.

- *The Creative Curriculum for Preschool* describes five ways in which families differ:

    structure

    personality

    temperament

    life experiences

    cultural differences

- In this workshop, you will assess how well you know the families of the children in your class or program. You will use what you know about each family to determine how you can best support them in helping their children develop language and literacy skills.

Show the transparency.

Write a fictitious name in column one. Describe the family below and fill in column two.

A single mother and her children live with their extended family who speak little English. The mother works afternoons and evenings so the children are cared for largely by grandparents.

Have participants name ways in which the teacher could involve the family and gain support for the child's literacy learning.

Possible responses:

Send home books in the family's primary language so the grandparents can share them with the child.

Share books that include references to the family's language or life experiences.

Invite the parent to tape record a story and send it to school for the child to listen to at choice time.

◀ ACTIVITY

Distribute the handout and give the following instructions:

- Write the name of each family in your classroom in column one, labeled "Family's Name."

- In column 2, record something unique you know about each family that may influence the type of support you offer. For example, a parent may be a non-reader or may not speak or read English. Or, perhaps there is a new baby in the family.

Stress that knowing every family's unique characteristics and circumstances enable teachers to communicate with, approach, and respond to each family in ways that make them feel respected and valued as a partner in their child's learning.

Ask participants to think about how this information might be used to build or strengthen a relationship and gain support for children's language and literacy learning. Have them record their ideas in column 3.

Allow time for participants to complete their forms. Invite a few people to share some of their ideas.

Point out the "Tips to Share With Families" on page 90 of *Literacy: The Creative Curriculum Approach*. Explain that each strategy discussed in Chapter 3 ends with "Tips to Share With Families."

Next, explain to participants that they will work together to generate ideas for a family lending library.

Have participants form pairs. Then give the following instructions:

- Select a favorite storybook and write a brief paragraph describing what the book is about. This is an example:

    From Head to Toe by Eric Carle is a simple story in which various animals challenge children to move their bodies in particular ways.

- Generate open-ended questions or comments family members could use while sharing the book with their children. Include some that could be used **before, during,** and **after** reading the book.

- Write at least one story-related activity a parent or family member could do with his or her child after the reading. Identify and/or design any additional materials needed to complete the activity. For example, a follow-up activity for *From Head to Toe* by Eric Carle might be this:

    After reading *From Head to Toe* by Eric Carle, have your child move a part of his or her body in the same ways pictured in the book. Invite your child to think of other ways to move.

Have the group determine the kind of container they will use for the books and related materials as well as their method for lending materials.

Note: If participants are from the same school or center, suggest that they gather or make materials and record the activities. Then assemble the story bags/boxes at a later workshop. If not, copy the ideas so participants can follow up on their own.

◀ SUMMARY

Summarize the workshop:

- Every family is different.

- Knowing and appreciating what is unique or different about each family helps you to build relationships and gain support that will foster children's learning and development.

- Families and teachers can work together to foster children's literacy learning.

Involving Families in Children's Literacy Learning

Family's Name	Something Special I Know About This Family	How I Can Use This Information to Build a Relationship and Support Children's Learning

3L22

Storytelling and Retelling

WORKSHOPS

🔑 Key Points	⬡ Workshop	📋 Materials	🕐 Time (minutes)
Storytelling is one of the oldest art forms. It can support children's literacy learning, contribute to their knowledge and understanding of the world, and promote their social and emotional well-being.	**Storytelling** (p. 106)	☐ Handout 3L23: Planning for Storytelling ☐ *Literacy*, pp. 47, 92–94, 102–103 ☐ Variation–Handout 3L24: Storytelling—*The Three Billy Goats Gruff*	45–60
Story retelling is one of the most effective strategies for developing and assessing children's comprehension skills and their understanding of story structure.	**Story Retelling** (p. 116)	☐ Handout 10F: Pattern—Caps ☐ Books, story props, newspaper, masking tape ☐ *Literacy*, pp. 101–107, 141–142	60–90

Storytelling

☐ Handout 3L23, p. 110
☐ Handout 3L24,
   pp. 111–115
☐ *Literacy*, pp. 47, 92–94,
   102–103

● PREPARATION

Choose a story to tell, preferably one that involves some level of audience participation. Prepare for the telling using the suggestions found on pages 92–94 of *Literacy: The Creative Curriculum Approach*. You may also consider using props as described on pages 102–103 of the same chapter.

A collection of books appropriate for storytelling (see descriptions on page 93 of *Literacy: The Creative Curriculum Approach*).

● INTRODUCTION

Introduce the workshop with a storytelling game that involves the whole group. Start the story then point to someone you would like to continue it. Continue until everyone has had a chance to contribute. This can also be done as table groups if the whole group is too large.

> "Once, not so very long ago, I was taking a walk in a nearby park when all of a sudden…"

Ask:

• How do children benefit from storytelling experiences such as this?

   Possible responses:

   They learn that language and storytelling are fun.

   They have to listen attentively.

   They learn to use animated, expressive, and descriptive language.

   Their creativity is enhanced.

   They learn how to follow a story line or carry on a story.

   They develop social skills as they work with others.

Make the following points:

- Storytelling is one of the oldest art forms and was once a common form of entertainment as well as a means of passing a culture's beliefs, values, and traditions from one generation to another.

- Many cultures still have a rich storytelling tradition.

- During this workshop, we will examine the ways in which storytelling promotes children's language and literacy learning as well as overall development.

Ask:

- How many of you consider yourselves storytellers?

- How many of you have ever used a phrase such as, "Once I...," or "Remember when...?" to recount an experience that was important to you?

Make the following points:

- Everyone is a storyteller. As human beings, we have a natural desire to express ourselves, share our life stories with others, and hear their stories.

- Even very young children eagerly tell their families, teachers, and friends about the latest events and experiences in their lives.

- The beauty of storytelling is that it requires no equipment, only the story and the imaginations of the storyteller and listeners.

- Like reading aloud, storytelling supports the development of many language and literacy skills and many other objectives of the Curriculum.

◀ ACTIVITY

Explain to participants that you have prepared a story to tell. Have them think about how telling the story would address the components of literacy as they listen or become involved.

Tell the story you have prepared. Invite participants to name ways in which storytelling supports each of the following:

- literacy as a source of enjoyment

- vocabulary and language

- phonological awareness

- understanding books

- knowledge of print

- comprehension

Have participants turn to the "Goals and Objectives at a Glance" in *Literacy: The Creative Curriculum Approach* (p. 47) and identify objectives from other areas of development that were addressed through this storytelling experience.

Make the following points:

- Storytelling is a valuable teaching tool and an enjoyable learning experience for children.

- For teachers, storytelling can be more challenging than reading aloud since the language and illustrations are not available to support the narration.

- *Literacy: The Creative Curriculum Approach* offers teachers specific guidance on how to begin telling stories.

- The more lively and engaging the story, the more valuable the experience is for the children.

Review and discuss the steps described on pages 92–94 including:

- Think of yourself as a storyteller

- Select appropriate stories

- Prepare for storytelling

Distribute the handout.

Have participants choose a book from the collection. Ask them to review and complete the handout. Invite them to take turns telling their stories to one another or the whole group.

SUMMARY

Summarize the workshop:

- In *Creative Curriculum* classrooms, children are offered opportunities to tell stories regularly—personal, real-life stories as well as those that have been read or told by their teachers and family members.

- Through preparation and practice, every teacher can become a skilled storyteller.

- And, with the appropriate support, children also become skilled storytellers.

VARIATION

Duplicate handout 3L24.

Have participants complete the handout writing the strategies the teacher uses to promote language and literacy skills in column 3.

Invite participants to share and discuss their ideas.

NOTES

Planning for Storytelling

Title of Book: _____

1. Why did you choose this book?

2. What background information about the story will you share with the children (e.g., type of story—folktale, fable, tall tale; origin; a story you remember from your childhood)?

3. Can children participate in the story? If so, how (e.g., reciting a repetitive a phrase, performing movements, or adding sound effects)?

4. List the characters. Then describe how you will portray each (e.g., consider tone, pitch, and volume of voice, movements, and actions).

5. How will you begin the story (e.g., consider the opening phrase, the setting, character descriptions)?

6. List the major events of the story in sequence.

7. How will you end the story?

Storytelling—
The Three Billy Goats Gruff

Ms. Tory places a globe, a toy troll, and a tone block in the Library Area. Then she invites the children to join her for a story.

Comments:

Ms. Tory:	*Today Mr. Alvarez and I are going to tell you a story. Since I won't be reading the story from a book and showing you the pictures, you will have to listen carefully to imagine what is happening in the story. Is everyone comfortable and ready to listen and think?* (Children nod their heads, yes.)
	The story is an old Norwegian folktale called The Three Billy Goats Gruff. A folktale is a story that people have told over and over and over again. In fact, this story has been told so many times we really aren't sure who the author is.
	When I was a little girl, my dad used to tell me stories that his dad told him. Now I tell the same stories to my son. Do any of your parents or grandparents tell you stories from long ago that someone else told them?
Carlos:	*My great-grandmother tells me stories about when she was a little girl in Mexico, before she came to America.*
Ms. Tory:	*Well, this story was first told in another country called Norway. Norway is far, far away, even farther away than Mexico. See? Here is where we live, and here is Norway.* (She uses a globe to show the children where Norway is in relation to their homes. Children comment on how far away Norway seems to be. Ms. Tory settles the children and then continues.)
	Does anyone know what a billy goat is?
Susie:	*A goat. Like the ones we saw at the farm.*
Ms. Tory:	*It is a goat. But what do you think a **billy** goat is?*

Storytelling—The Three Billy Goats Gruff, continued

Juwan: *I have a friend named Billy.*

Ms. Tory: *Is your friend a boy?* (Juwan nods his head, yes.) *That might give you a hint.* (Ms. Tory pauses and waits for a child to respond. She continues.) *Even though some girls are named Billie, a billy goat is a male, or boy, goat. So this is a story about three boy goats. Let's begin.*

Ms. Tory: *Once upon a time, in a land far away, there lived three billy goats. And the last name of all three billy goats was Gruff.*

Ms. Tory: *The youngest billy goat Gruff was very, very small. He had two little horns just starting to show on the top of his head and he spoke in a soft voice.* (Each time Ms. Tory introduces a new character, she changes the pitch of her voice and uses her hands to show the size of the goats and its horns.)

The second billy goat Gruff was a middle-sized goat. He had horns, too, and he had a few whiskers on his chin.

The last and oldest was great big billy goat Gruff. He was HUGE! He had long, pointed horns, almost like spears; big hooves; and a beard. He made his two brothers feel safe because he was so big and strong.

Ben: *My brother Broderick is strong!*

Ms. Tory: *Does anyone remember what billy goats like to eat?*

Zach: *Grass and seeds.*

Carlos: *And sometimes old shoes and stuff like that!*

Storytelling—The Three Billy Goats Gruff, continued

Ms. Tory: *Well, these billy goats loved to eat sweet, green, juicy grass more than anything else. One day when they were grazing on grass near their home, one of them noticed a lush hillside not too far away. The grass looked green and tasty, and, when the breeze blew, the goats could smell its sweet smell. They just had to have it, so they decided to go up to the hillside to get some of the grass.*

But…(Ms. Tory pauses and looks in the children's eyes.) *there was a problem. You see, to get to the other hillside, the billy goats had to cross a bridge. Now the bridge wasn't the problem, but what lived under the bridge was a BIG problem.*

What do you think lived under the bridge?

Children: *A monster!*

Ms. Tory: (Ms. Tory lowers her voice, moves a little closer to the children, and speaks slowly and deliberately.) *Under the bridge lived a TROLL.* (Ms. Tory takes out a toy troll and shows it to the children.) *This is a toy troll. But the troll that lived under the bridge was BIG and UGLY and VERY, VERY MEAN!*

His eyes were as big as saucers, so he could spot a goat a mile away. And his nose was as long as a poker, which meant he could smell a goat a mile away. (Mr. Alvarez stands nearby and makes gestures to indicate the size and nature of the troll.)

Kate: *He would scare me! He's so big and mean and ugly!*

Ben: *Yeah! I bet he gets the billy goats when they cross the bridge. Huh, Ms. Tory?*

Storytelling—The Three Billy Goats Gruff, continued

Ms. Tory: *Well, the first billy goat to cross the bridge was the small billy goat Gruff. He went trip-trap, trip-trap, trip-trap over the bridge.* (Ms. Tory uses the tone block to make faint, fast, trotting hoof sounds.)

About that time the troll roars in the meanest, loudest voice you've ever heard.

Mr. Alvarez: *Who's that tripping over my bridge?* (Clenches his fist and uses a deep, roaring voice.)

Ms. Tory: (Responds in a quivering, high-pitched voice.) *It is I, the tiniest billy goat Gruff. I'm going to the hillside to make myself fat.*

Mr. Alvarez: *I'm coming to gobble you up!*

Ms. Tory: (Again in a tiny, pleading voice.) *Oh, no! Please don't take me. I'm much too little. Wait for my brother, the middle-size billy goat Gruff. He's much bigger and meatier than I am.*

Mr. Alvarez: *Very well. Be off with you!*

Susie: *That billy goat tricked you!* (Points to Mr. Alvarez.)

Mr. Alvarez: *You're right. I may need some help!* (Invites children to participate.) *Let me hear you say, in your meanest troll voices, "Now I'm coming to gobble you* up!" (Children respond.)

The story continues with Ms. Tory playing the part of each billy goat and Mr. Alvarez playing the troll. To represent the difference in the size and strength of each goat, she plays the tone block more and more slowly, loudly, and deliberately, and she alters the pitch, tone, and volume of her voice.

Storytelling—The Three Billy Goats Gruff, continued

Ms. Tory: *Pretty soon, all three billy goats were on the hillside eating that sweet, juicy, green grass. They ate so much that they got really, really fat and they could hardly make it home. In fact, they are probably still fat. And so— snip, snap, snout—this tale's told out.*

What did you think about that story?

Children: *It was good! That big billy goat wasn't afraid of the troll.*

At first I was scared! But I'm not now.

Ms. Tory: *It can be a little scary. Do you think that story really happened or do you think it was make-believe?*

Carlos: *Make-believe, because goats don't really talk.*

Ben: *And there is no such thing as a troll.*

Ms. Tory affirms their responses and continues the discussion. She asks the children if they would like to hear the story again. She and Mr. Alvarez make plans to create puppets and a backdrop to use next time. After that, they will invite the children to retell the story using the props, and they will add the props to the Library Area for the children to use at choice time.

Story Retelling

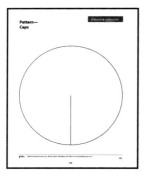

☐ Handout 10F, p. 119
☐ Books, story props, newspaper, masking tape
☐ *Literacy*, pp. 101–107, 141–142

PREPARATION

Review the pages indicated in *Literacy: The Creative Curriculum Approach*.

Make the peddlers' caps out of felt (white, red, blue, gray, and brown) using the pattern on handout 10F. Cut 1 white felt circle and use a permanent marker to make it checked. Slit the circle on the dotted line. Overlap the edges and secure them with fabric glue or sew them together. Cut equal numbers of caps from the other pieces of colored felt. Make enough so that every person in the workshop can "steal" a cap from the peddler.

Gather a collection of favorite books you might use in retelling experiences with children. Either bring these or ask the program sponsor to collect them ahead of time.

Collect the materials listed for small-group work.

INTRODUCTION

Introduce the workshop:

• Research tells us that comprehension skills are essential to a child's future reading success (Teale and Yokota, 2000).

• Instruction that builds comprehension skills should be a central part of teaching young children about reading.

• Research confirms that story retelling is one of the most effective strategies for developing and assessing children's comprehension and their understanding of story structure.

ACTIVITY

Read the story *Caps for Sale* by Esphyr Slobodkina. Then follow these procedures.

Explain to participants that you would like to involve them in retelling the story and then discuss the value of the experience.

Ask for a volunteer to play the peddler. Give the volunteer the caps.

Ask everyone else to play a monkey.

Retell the story, acting as the narrator.

Debrief the retelling experience.

Include a discussion about the teacher's role and offering varying levels of support.

Ask participants to consider ways in which story retelling addresses the other components of literacy including: vocabulary and language development; phonological awareness; literacy as a source of enjoyment; and books and other texts.

Have them think about ways in which story retelling supports learning in other areas of development.

Have participants read the scenario on retelling on pages 104–107 of *Literacy: The Creative Curriculum Approach*. Discuss the strategies the teachers used to support children's retelling of the story.

Have participants form small groups and work together to demonstrate various retelling strategies. Use one of the two activities that follow:

1. Assign a retelling activity from *Literacy: The Creative Curriculum Approach*. Provide the materials necessary for one of the following:

   A Bunny's Tale

   Clothesline Storytelling

   Listening Cords

   Pocket Storytelling: *The Mitten*

2. Have each group select a book. Have them create story retelling props using only newspaper and masking tape.

Invite each group to share/demonstrate its ideas.

SUMMARY

Summarize the workshop:

- Story retelling provides children the opportunity to actively participate in a literacy experience.

- Story retelling promotes language and literacy skills as well as other social/emotional, physical, and cognitive skills.

- The Library Area is the ideal place for children to continue exploring language and literacy through retelling experiences.

NOTES

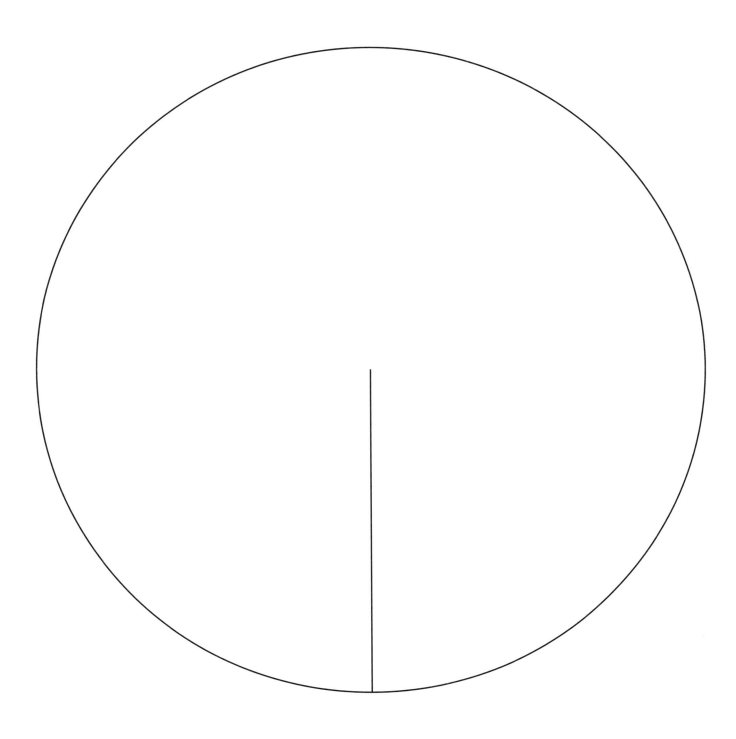

10F

Writing

WORKSHOPS

○ Key Points	✿ Workshop	▤ Materials	🕐 Time (minutes)
Reading and writing are interrelated. Therefore, writing should be an integral part of the preschool literacy program.	**The Value of Writing** (p. 122)	☐ *Creative Curriculum* video ☐ Handout 3L25: Writing Scenario ☐ *Literacy*, pp.111–113 ☐ *Creative Curriculum*, pp. 359–360 ☐ Chart paper, markers	30–45
Children reveal what they know about written language through their independent writing. With this knowledge, teachers can plan activities and experiences to help children make progress in their learning.	**Using Writing to Assess Children's Literacy Learning** (p. 130)	☐ Handout 3L26: Writing Samples ☐ *Literacy*, pp. 22–24, 137–138, Appendix	30–45

The Value of Writing

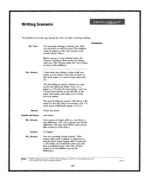

☐ *Creative Curriculum* video
☐ Handout 3L25, p. 126–129
☐ *Literacy*, pp.111–113
☐ *Creative Curriculum*, pp. 359–360
☐ Chart paper, markers

PREPARATION

Cue the *Creative Curriculum* video to the Blocks segment that shows how a child uses writing to record the solution to a problem.

Duplicate the handout.

Write the name of each interest area at the top of a piece of chart paper. Post the charts around the room.

INTRODUCTION

Introduce the workshop by showing the Blocks segment from *The Creative Curriculum* video. Pose the following questions:

- What did the children in the video know about print and writing?

  Possible responses:

  Print is meaningful. It carries a message.

  Print serves a purpose or function.

  We can communicate thoughts and ideas through writing.

  Print can be read by others.

  A name represents ownership or identity.

  A sign serves as a type of label.

  They have a notion of what writing looks like.

- What role did the teacher play?

  Possible responses:

  She encouraged the children to use oral and written language to solve a social problem.

  She provided materials.

  She set the stage for children to use writing for a purpose.

  She accepted the child's writing as a meaningful form of communication.

- How do you think the children might have learned about print, and more specifically, writing?

  Possible responses:

  They saw family members or peers writing.

  The teacher wrote often with the children in the classroom.

  They heard adults talk about what they were doing and why as they wrote.

  The children had opportunities to explore and experiment with writing on their own.

Discuss the implications for classroom practice. Make the following points:

- Teachers and other adults play a key role in helping children learn about written language.

- Children need time and opportunities to observe and interact with adults and peers in authentic reading and writing experiences.

- Children need time and opportunities to explore and experiment with written language on their own.

- Research confirms that reading and writing are interactive and interrelated processes. Therefore, writing should be an integral part of the preschool literacy program.

- The purpose of this workshop is to explore ways in which writing is used to promote children's literacy learning intentionally and address the components of literacy.

◖ **ACTIVITY**

Distribute the handout. Have participants read the writing scenario to identify the skills and components of literacy the teacher addresses intentionally. Have them record their ideas in column 3.

Invite participants to share their ideas.

Lead a discussion about the teacher's role. Use these points and activities to guide your discussion:

- Teachers must plan for a variety of writing experiences.

- One of the first and most important things children can learn about written language is that it is meaningful and serves a function or purpose.

- Print carries a message and is therefore used to accomplish many tasks.

Have participants brainstorm with others at their tables to create a list of the writing experiences they offer in their preschool classrooms. Tell them to consider various events of the day (e.g. arrival/departure, attendance, large- and small-group times, snack and meal time, choice time, routines and transitions, outdoors).

Next, have them go back through their lists to identify what children could learn about the functions of print through each of the experiences. Offer an example if necessary.

Possible responses:

Experience	Function
Writing names	*To show ownership or express identity*
Taking dictation	*To express their ideas, thoughts, feeling, opinions*
Making lists	*To satisfy a need (recall information) or desire*
Writing recipes	*To tell others how to do something*
Journal writing	*To express their ideas, thoughts, feeling, opinions*
Messages and notes	*To communicate with others*
Creating signs and labels	*To tell others what to do*
Writing letters and cards	*To communicate with others*
Making books	*To express themselves creatively*

Refer participants to pages 111–113 of *Literacy: The Creative Curriculum Approach* and review the list of planned writing experiences described.

Make the following points:

- For many children, print is not a part of their everyday experiences, so they do not view writing as a useful tool.

- In a *Creative Curriculum* classroom, teachers plan authentic writing experiences for various events of the day. In this way, children learn that written language is used for multiple purposes and can satisfy many needs.

Introduce the idea that teachers must model writing and talk naturally about the functions, forms, and conventions of print as they write.

Explain that children's ability to write develops over time.

Refer participants back to the scenario. Lead a discussion about the things Mr. Alvarez did intentionally:

- He described his actions and thinking, explaining the purpose for writing, calling attention to features and forms of letters and words, as well as letter sounds.

- He demonstrated the uses of print, left-to-right directionality, letter formation, and speech-to-word correspondence.

- He asked open-ended questions and acknowledged the children's responses.

- He helped children make connections.

- He involved children in the activity.

Explain that children need time, opportunities, and materials to experiment with writing and explore different ways to convey messages in print.

Have participants reflect on ways in which they encourage writing in interest areas. Have them do a "walk about" recording their ideas on the charts posted around the room. Explain that they can not write something that has already been listed.

Debrief the activity. Make the following points:

- Children should have access to writing materials in every interest area so they can try out the ideas they have formed about writing during their observations of and interactions with others.

- In a *Creative Curriculum* classroom, the Library Area is the primary place where children explore writing. On pages 359–360 of *The Creative Curriculum for Preschool*, you will find an extensive list of writing materials appropriate for the Library Area.

- The Dramatic Play Area is the second area where reading and writing are used extensively. Here children explore real-world situations in which reading and writing are useful.

If time permits, have participants form small groups, choose a dramatic play topic (e.g., shoe store, florists, bank, dentist's/doctor's office) and brainstorm literacy props (writing and reading) that could be added to enhance children's dramatic play.

Invite each group to share a few of their ideas. Have a volunteer type the lists and distribute them to each participant at the next workshop.

SUMMARY

Summarize the workshop:

- Young children enjoy the process of writing, the social relationships they develop during the process, and the sense of accomplishment they feel as they express themselves through writing.

- Like reading, writing experiences are an integral part of the day in every *Creative Curriculum* classroom.

Writing Scenario

The children sit on the rug, facing Ms. Tory for their morning meeting.

Comments:

Ms. Tory:	*Our morning meeting is almost over. Who can tell what we will do next?* (The children recite in unison as Ms. Tory points to the words Choice Time.)
	Before you go to your interest areas, Mr. Alvarez is going to share some new things with you. (Mr. Alvarez takes Ms. Tory's place in front of the children.)
Mr. Alvarez:	*I have three new things to share with you today. Let me make a short list of them on this chart paper so I won't forget what they are.*
	The first thing we need to discuss is a new toy for the Sand and Water Area. It's a pump, so I'll write the word pump. *Let's see, I'll start here* (points to the left side of the paper and names each letter as he writes) p-u-m-p, pump.
	The second thing we need to talk about is the snack for the day. Since I'm writing a list, I'll write snack *underneath* pump: s-n-a-c-k.
Shawn:	*That's my name!*
Setsuko and Sonya:	*And mine!*
Mr. Alvarez:	*Your names do begin with an* s, *but there is one difference. Let's see if anyone can tell the difference.* (He says each child's name aloud; then writes it on the chart.)
Jonetta:	*It's bigger!*
Mr. Alvarez:	*You are watching closely, Jonetta. Their names begin with a capital, or uppercase* S, *and the word* snack *begins with a lowercase* s. *The letters are formed the same way, but they are different sizes. See?* (Mr. Alvarez writes* Ss *so the children can see the difference.)

From *Literacy: The Creative Curriculum® Approach*
©2005 Teaching Strategies, Inc., PO Box 42243, Washington, DC 20015; www.TeachingStrategies.com

3L25

126

Writing Scenario, continued

Setsuko: *I have both.*

Mr. Alvarez: *You certainly do, Setsuko. A capital* S *at the beginning of your name and a lowercase* s *in the middle of your name.* (Mr. Alvarez draws a line under each *s* as he speaks.)

The third thing I would like to share is the set of pictures from our trip to the apple orchard. Let's see. What should I write?

Malik: *How about pictures?*

Mr. Alvarez: *What do the rest of you think?* (The children nod their heads, yes.) *Pictures.* (Mr. Alvarez repeats the word as he writes it on the chart.) *Hey,* pictures *and* pump *start with the same letter,* p.

(Mr. Alvarez returns to the top of the list and reads *pump*.) *Have you ever seen a pump before? Can you guess what it does?* (He takes the pump from a nearby box and explains that a pump is a tool that people use to help move water from one place to another. He has prepared a tub of water so he can demonstrate how it works. The children ask several questions and take turns pumping the handle. Mr. Alvarez records their questions on chart paper and repeats their words as he writes.)

Mr. Alvarez: *You've asked some very interesting questions, and I bet you'll discover some of the answers when you work with the pump in the Sand and Water Area. I've written your questions on the chart so we can come back and talk more about them at our next meeting. We need to create a pegboard label for the pump so you will know where to put it when you are finished using it.* (Mr. Alvarez has cut a picture of the pump from a catalog and glued it on card stock. Together they create a label. He talks as he writes p-u-m-p.)

(He reads the word slowly, sweeping his hand under the word.) *Does anyone notice anything special about the word* pump?

Writing Scenario, continued

Alexa: *It has two of the same letter.*

Mr. Alvarez: *That's right, Alexa. It has two ps, one at the beginning of the word and one at the end. Listen and you'll hear the sound that the letter* p *makes.* (He reads the word slowly again to call attention to the /p/ sounds in the word.) *I'll put this label on the pegboard in the Sand and Water Area, along with the pump. Be sure to try it when you work there today.*

I'll cross out the word pump *now, because we have talked about it.*

Mr. Alvarez and children: (Mr. Alvarez looks at the list again, then takes the snack menu out of the box. He holds it so all the children can see.) *Today's snack is Trail Mix. You will have an opportunity to make your own trail mix in the Cooking Area.*

Let's look at the recipe and read the list of ingredients. (He holds up a picture/ word recipe made with labels from familiar food products. He sweeps his hand under the words.) *Cheerios, pretzels, raisins, almonds.* (The children call the almonds *nuts.* He explains that almonds are one type of nut and points out the word *Almonds* on the package. He continues to read the directions with the children and tells them that the recipe will be posted for them to follow.)

Mr. Alvarez: *Who remembers what to do if you want to prepare snack but the Cooking Area is too crowded?*

Zack: *Write your name on the snack sign-up sheet.*

Writing Scenario, continued

Mr. Alvarez: *Zack, will you show everyone the sign-up sheet?* (Zack shows the children the new sign-up sheet for the day, and Mr. Alvarez reminds them that the sign-up sheet helps to make sure that everyone has a turn to make snack. He reminds them to cross their names off of the list when they have finished preparing snack and to let the next person on the list know it is her turn.

Let me cross snack *off our list.* (He draws a line through the word.)

Do you remember the third thing we need to talk about? (He points to the word *pictures* on the list.)

All children: *Pictures*! (Mr. Alvarez takes a photo album out of the box and shows a few pictures to the children.)

Mr. Alvarez: *I'm going to put these in the Library Area for you to look at. I'll be visiting the Area today so you can dictate a few sentences about the pictures. That way, your families will be able to read about all the things that happened on our trip to the apple orchard.*

(Puts a line through the word *pictures*.) *That's the last thing on our list. I think it's time for you to choose the Area in which you want to play.*

Using Writing to Assess Children's Literacy Learning

□ Handout 3L26,
   pp. 133–143
□ *Literacy*, pp. 22–24,
   137–138, Appendix

◀ PREPARATION

Duplicate the writing samples so each table will have a collection or collect samples from the children in your program that reflect various levels of understanding of print and stages of writing development. Refer to pages 22–24 and 137–138 *Literacy: The Creative Curriculum Approach*.

◀ INTRODUCTION

Introduce the workshop:

- When children have opportunities to write as part of everyday activities, they try out their ideas and experiment with written language.

- Through writing, children reveal what they know about the functions, forms, and conventions of print.

- The purpose of this workshop is to examine samples of children's writing to practice assessing their writing development and understanding of print concepts.

- Teachers who are familiar with the sequence of development for writing will be able to plan activities and experiences that will help children progress.

ACTIVITY

Have participants review the information about knowledge of print on pages 22–24 and the developmental steps in writing on pages 137–138 of *Literacy: The Creative Curriculum Approach*.

Have them review the steps on the *Developmental Continuum* for objectives 45, 46, 49, and 50 found in the Appendix of *Literacy: The Creative Curriculum Approach*.

Distribute the writing samples.

Give these directions:

- Work together to identify each child's knowledge and understanding of written language based on their writing samples and the steps of the *Developmental Continuum* objectives.

- Identify what you might do or say to help further each child's progress.

Lead a discussion about the writing samples with the entire group. Invite participants to share their comments and observations.

Refer participants to the Observation Forms in the Appendix. Explain that these forms may be used with *The Creative Curriculum Developmental Continuum* Assessment System to further clarify and document children's literacy learning.

SUMMARY

Summarize the workshop:

- Each child is at a different level in terms of his literacy learning.

- Through observation of children and analysis of their work samples, teachers can determine what children know about written language and what reading and writing skills they possess.

- This information enables teachers to plan for and guide children's learning more effectively.

NOTES

Writing Samples

Rachel's Drawing for Ryan

Rachel said to Ryan, "I'm going to draw a picture for you."

This is what she drew and wrote.

Jacqueline's Self Portrait

Jacqueline drew a self portrait.

She asked a class visitor if she had a child. The visitor said, "Yes, a son." Jacqueline drew a picture and asked the visitor how to spell her son's name. Jacqueline wrote each letter as the visitor named it (Chris).

Writing Samples, continued

Steven's Picture of Minnie Mouse

Writing Samples, continued

Cecelia's Letter

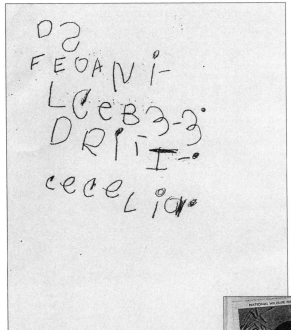

Looking at her letter, Cecelia read aloud:

Dear Ashley,

If I'm not home, I am at my Grandma's.

Cecelia

She put the letter in an envelope, addressed it, then put it in Ashley's mailbox.

Terry's Card

Terry's wrote a card to his Dad.
He read pointing to each word:

Dad. You're great.

Terry

Writing Samples, continued

Steven's Drawing of an Airport

When asked about the stop sign, Steven explained that it had to be there to tell the pilots when they needed to stop the plane.

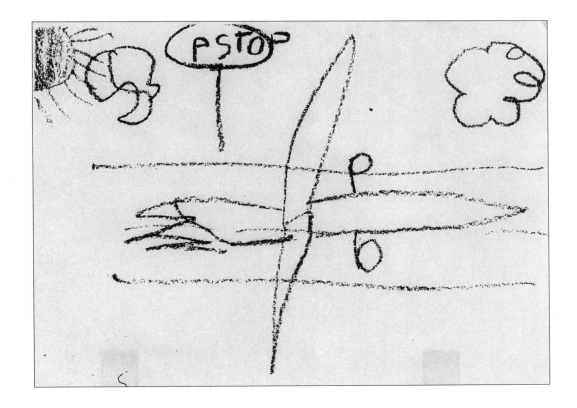

Writing Samples, continued

Tina's Shopping List

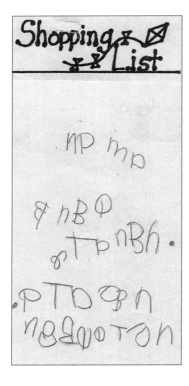

Tina was in the Dramatic Play Area when she made the list and then read it to her teacher.

Eggs

Ice cream

Cherries

Potato chips

Bubble gum

Writing Samples, continued

Kacie's Letter

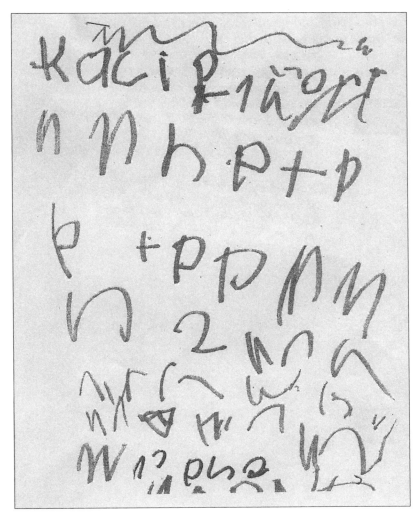

Kacie said, "I wrote a letter. Do you want me to read it?"

Looking at the letter she read:

"I love you Mom and Dad. I wish you would come pick me up. I have fun at school. I write 1, 2, 3. I learn my ABCs. I'm ready to go to kindergarten. I love my Nanna. Kacie"

Writing Samples, continued

Emily's Note

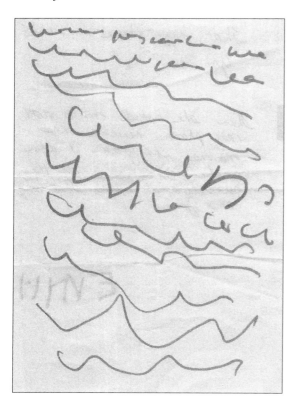

Emily wrote and handed the paper to a visitor. She said, "That's my phone number. You call me."

She asked the visitor to write her phone number and name. She wrote and gave the paper to Emily. Emily folded it, scribbled on the outside, and then pointed and said, "That says Ms. Jones."

Writing Samples, continued

Jinci's Letter

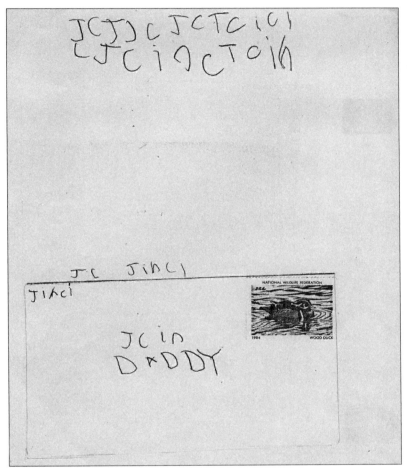

Jinci's letter to her Dad with the envelope she addressed.

Writing Samples, continued

Chris's Drawing

This is a page from Chris's book about dinosaurs.

Writing Samples, continued

Crystal's Drawing

Crystal drew a picture of fish. She asked her teacher to write the word "fish" at the top of her paper. She signed her name, then copied the word "fish."

Playing: Children's Work

WORKSHOPS

⚲ Key Points	✸ Workshop	📄 Materials	🕐 Time (minutes)
Play is an effective vehicle for learning language and literacy skills.	**Linking Literacy and Play** (p. 146)	☐ Open-ended classroom materials (e.g., puzzles, Legos, beads, etc.) ☐ *Literacy*, p. 148	20
Teachers' interactions with children during their play are critical to language and literacy development.	**The Teacher's Role During Play** (p. 148)	☐ Transparency 3L27: Teacher Roles in Supporting Play (5 pages) ☐ *Miss Tizzy* by Libba Moore Gray ☐ Literacy materials (e.g., books, environmental print, magnetic letters, writing materials, story props, etc.) ☐ *Literacy*, pp. 122–125	20
Teachers provide optimal support for literacy learning when they observe children's play and offer literacy props, ideas, and suggestions that extend, rather than interfere, with play.	**Promoting Literacy Through Play** (p. 156)	☐ Handout 3L28: Promoting Literacy Through Play ☐ Variation–Handout 3L29: Promoting Literacy Through Play—Scenarios	30
The types of questions or statements teachers make lead children to build language and literacy skills.	**Guiding Language and Literacy Development With Open-Ended Questions** (p. 160)	☐ Handout 3L30: Building Language Using Open-Ended Questions ☐ *Literacy*, pp. 133–189 ☐ Common classroom materials (e.g., puzzles, Legos, beads, etc.) ☐ Literacy-related materials (e.g., books, environmental print, storytelling props, writing materials, letter and word manipulatives, etc.)	20
The *Developmental Continuum* helps guide instruction in language and literacy.	**Using Assessment Information to Guide Literacy Learning** (p. 164)	☐ Handout 3L31: Planning for Antonia ☐ Handout 3L31-Trainer: Planning for Antonia ☐ Literacy materials (e.g., books, environmental print, magnetic letters, writing materials, story props, etc.) ☐ *Literacy*, Appendix	30

Linking Literacy and Play

□ Open-ended
classroom materials
(e.g., puzzles, Legos,
beads, etc.)
□ *Literacy*, p. 148

PREPARATION

Gather materials that children use in interest areas regularly such as puzzles, collage materials, clay, Legos, a collection of nature items.

Assemble a different set of materials for each small group of participants.

INTRODUCTION

Introduce the workshop:

- Play is an important part of young children's lives. During play, children explore and construct their understandings about the world.

- As the demands for accountability increase, literacy instruction and play appear to be competing for the teacher's time and attention. And, many people do not see the significance of children's play as it relates to language and literacy.

- Play and literacy learning are not exclusive experiences. Numerous studies show the link between play and language and literacy development.

- Environments that include rich and diverse materials nourish children's language and literacy development. Teachers within these environments respond to children's explorations to scaffold their learning.

- The purposes of this workshop are to increase your awareness of the value of play as a teaching strategy and to help you learn to explain how literacy skills are learned through play.

- In this workshop, you will look at the value of materials that are not specific to literacy and see how they can enhance skills in language and literacy development.

ACTIVITY

Have participants turn to page 148 of *Literacy: The Creative Curriculum Approach* and review the chart. Make the following remarks:

- This chart shows how everyday play experiences are linked to literacy development.

- If you can articulate how children are learning literacy skills as they play, you are able to explain the value of children's play to others.

Have participants form small groups.

Give each group a set of materials that children typically play with in a preschool classroom.

Have them discuss each material and identify the literacy skills a child might develop while using it. Have them record their ideas on chart paper and post it on the wall.

When everyone is finished, have the participants walk about to review the charts or invite each group to share their ideas about a particular material.

Invite participants to share any observations about this experience or ways in which they could share this information with families and others.

Point out that each interest area section in *Literacy: The Creative Curriculum Approach* begins with a chart describing ways in which everyday play experiences promote language and literacy development.

Invite participants to examine the chart at the beginning of an interest area chapter in the book.

SUMMARY

Summarize the workshop:

- Many of the materials found in an early childhood classroom are not ones that you typically think of as language and literacy materials.

- Through this experience, you learned how everyday materials can contribute to children's language and literacy development.

- Now you can share this information with families and those who don't understand the value of play or more specifically the way in which play supports children's oral language, reading, and writing development.

The Teacher's Role During Play

Teacher Roles in
Supporting Play

Observer

Facilitor

Player

Leader

☐ Transparency 3L27,
  pp. 151–155
☐ *Miss Tizzy*
☐ Literacy materials (e.g.,
  books, environmental
  print, magnetic letters,
  writing materials, story
  props, etc.)
☐ *Literacy*, pp. 122–125

◖ PREPARATION

Prepare the five pages of the transparency.

Become familiar with *Miss Tizzy* by Libba Moore Gray.

Assemble sets of literacy materials (e.g., books, magnetic letters, flannel board stories, alphabet bingo, name cards, paper and markers, chalkboards and chalk, environmental print), one set for each group of four people.

◖ INTRODUCTION

Introduce the workshop by reading *Miss Tizzy*. Ask participants to think about the following questions as you read:

*   What type of relationship did Miss Tizzy have with the neighborhood children?

*   What roles did Miss Tizzy play?

*   What kind of environment did Miss Tizzy create for the children?

Lead a discussion about the story. Make the following points:

*   In a *Creative Curriculum* classroom, teachers create an environment where children feel safe and free to explore, experiment, and try out their ideas.

*   Teachers get to know children by observing and interacting with them during play. They follow the children's lead and provide support on varying levels.

*   To support children's literacy learning during play appropriately, teachers must assume multiple roles, as Miss Tizzy did.

Show the first page of the transparency with the four roles.

Explain that teachers function in many different ways:

- They observe—offer encouragement or validate children's efforts.

- They facilitate—offer props or assistance to help children get their play started.

- They play—participate in a play theme at the invitation of the children. Through dialogue, or literacy activities related to the play, children's literacy learning is extended.

- They lead—intentionally introduce a new literacy-related idea into children's existing play.

Explain to participants that the purpose of this workshop is to explore these four roles more fully so they can guide children's learning during play more effectively.

ACTIVITY

Have the participants form groups of four. Give each group a set of literacy materials.

Have each person in the groups choose a number 1, 2, 3, or 4. This will identify the round of play in which each will assume the teacher's role.

1. Observer
2. Facilitator
3. Player
4. Leader

Explain the activity:

- There will be four rounds of play.

- Prior to each round, everyone will read the respective play scenario described on pages 122–125 of *Literacy: The Creative Curriculum Approach*.

- After the reading, one of you will assume the teacher's role while the rest of you will play the role of children using the materials on your table.

- You will not be acting out the scenarios in the book. Instead you will participate in scenes similar to those described in the book. The goal is to learn more about different roles and different levels of interaction you can offer to promote children's literacy learning. I will display a transparency page to remind you of each teacher role.

Round 1: (display appropriate transparency)
Children use the props to act out familiar, everyday roles.
Teacher observes children's play, offers encouragement, or validates children's efforts.

Round 2: (display appropriate transparency)
Children choose a dramatic play topic (e.g., doctor's office, florist, garage, florist).
Teacher facilitates play by providing props and materials or helping children arrange
an area for a particular kind of play.

Round 3: (display appropriate transparency)
Children choose a dramatic play topic. Invite the teacher to play with you.
Teacher participates in the children's play when invited. Try to enhance or expand
the children's literacy learning by talking about or using literacy activities related
to the play topic.

Round 4: (display appropriate transparency)
Children use the props to act out familiar, everyday roles.
Teacher intentionally introduces new literacy ideas in thoughtful, respectful ways.

Invite the participants to share their thoughts about the play experiences. Ask:

- Which roles were more challenging? Why?

- What does it mean to follow the child's lead? Was this difficult to do?

◀ SUMMARY

Summarize the workshop:

- The way in which you interact with children during their play is critical to their
  language and literacy development.

- Skilled teachers observe children as they play and then offer an appropriate level
  of support. If enough support is not given, then learning opportunities are missed.
  If too much support is given or teachers are intrusive, children's play may be stifled
  or higher levels of thinking and learning may not occur.

Teacher Roles in Supporting Play

Observer

Facilitor

Player

Leader

3L27

Round 1

Children:
Use the props to act out familiar, everyday roles.

Teacher:
Observe the children's play and offer encouragement through a smile or nod of the head, or validate a child's effort.

Round 2

Children:
Choose a dramatic play topic and begin your play.

Teacher:
Support the children by providing props and materials or helping them arrange an area for a particular kind of play. Do *not* participate in the play.

Round 3

Children:
Choose a dramatic play topic and invite the teacher to play with you.

Teacher:
Participate in the children's play at their invitation. Assume a role or character, extend the children's play through dialogue or literacy activities related to the play theme.

Round 4

Children:
Use the props to act out familiar, everyday roles.

Teacher:
Direct aspects of the children's play, not by controlling the play, but by intentionally introducing new ideas.

3L27

Promoting Literacy Through Play

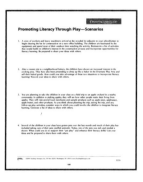

☐ Handout 3L28, p. 158
☐ Variation–Handout
   3L29, p. 159

PREPARATION

Duplicate the handout.

INTRODUCTION

Introduce the activity:

- In a previous workshop you learned about the four roles teachers assume during children's play episodes: observer, facilitator, player, and leader.

- In this workshop you will look at play episodes from a classroom and consider ways you can promote literacy without interrupting the children's play.

Give the following instructions:

- Form groups of three or four people.

- Think of a play episode from your classroom. Try to recall one in which the children were deeply involved and engaged. Share it with your group.

- Label each box on handout 3L28 with a title of one of the play episodes, e.g., "Digging Holes" or "Birthday Party." (You may choose to do this on chart paper instead.)

- Work together and come up with ways that you could enhance each play experience with literacy learning. Record your ideas on the handout.

Allow about 20 minutes for groups to complete their work.

Now ask half of the participants to discuss their lists in terms of the seven components of literacy and the other half to think about the literacy experiences in light of the seven teaching strategies.

Debrief by asking:

- Were all of the components of literacy addressed in your play experiences?

- Which components seemed to predominate? Which were not addressed?

- Were all of the teaching strategies addressed in your play experiences?

- Which teaching strategies seemed to predominate? Which were not addressed?

SUMMARY

Summarize the workshop:

- Play enables children to use literacy skills in a meaningful way.

- Teachers provide optimal support for literacy learning when they observe children in their play and offer literacy props, ideas, and suggestions. In this way teachers do not interrupt children's play, but rather extend the play.

VARIATION

Duplicate and distribute handout 3L29.

Have participants form small groups of four.

Assign or ask each to choose a scenario described on the handout. Make sure all scenarios are addressed by at least one group.

Explain that they are to read their scenario and work together to identify ways literacy could be incorporated into the experience, and specifically into play activities surrounding the experience.

Have participants record their ideas on the handout. Allow about 20-30 minutes for groups to complete their work.

After the groups are finished, have them examine their lists to determine which components of literacy are addressed and which teaching strategies are used.

Promoting Literacy Through Play

Play Description:

How I can incorporate literacy:

Play Description:

How I can incorporate literacy:

Play Description:

How I can incorporate literacy:

Play Description:

How I can incorporate literacy:

3L28

Promoting Literacy Through Play—Scenarios

1. A crew of workers and heavy machinery arrived at the wooded lot adjacent to your school/center to begin clearing the lot for construction on a new office building. The children are fascinated by the equipment and spend most of their outdoor time watching the activity. Brainstorm a list of activities that would build on children's interest in the construction process and incorporate opportunities for literacy learning. Be prepared to share your ideas with others.

2. After a recent trip to a neighborhood bakery, the children have shown an increased interest in the cooking area. They have also been pretending to dress up like a baker in the Dramatic Play Area and sell their baked goods. How could you take advantage of these two situations to incorporate literacy learning? Record your ideas to share with others.

3. You are planning to take the children in your class on a field trip to an apple orchard in a nearby community. In addition to picking apples, they will see how other people make their living from apples. They will visit several local merchants and sample products such as apple juice, applesauce, apple butter, and other products. As you think about planning the trip, taking the trip, and any follow-up play activities, consider ways in which you could involve the children to integrate literacy learning. Generate a list of ideas to share with others.

4. Several of the children in your class have gotten pets over the last month and much of their play has included taking care of their pets (stuffed animals). Today, one of the pets was sick and needed a doctor. What could you do to support their "pet play" and enhance their literacy skills? List your ideas and be prepared to share them with others.

WORKSHOP

Guiding Language and Literacy Development With Open-Ended Questions

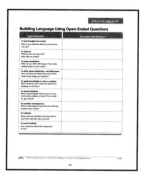

☐ Handout 3L30, p. 163
☐ *Literacy*, pp. 133–189
☐ Common classroom materials (e.g., puzzles, Legos, beads, etc.)
☐ Literacy-related materials (e.g., books, environmental print, storytelling props, writing materials, letter and word manipulatives, etc.)

PREPARATION

Duplicate the handout.

Gather common classroom and literacy-related materials.

INTRODUCTION

Introduce the workshop:

- The types of questions or statements you make lead children to engage in conversations with you which build language skills.

- The purpose of this workshop is to explore ways you can enrich a child's oral vocabulary as well as critical thinking skills by asking open-ended questions during play.

- Open-ended questions are questions that can be answered in a number of different ways.

ACTIVITY

Assign each table a different interest area and distribute the handout. Ask the participants to locate their interest area section in Chapter 4 of *Literacy: The Creative Curriculum Approach*. Provide the following instructions:

- Handout 3L30 defines different types of open-ended questions along with an example of each one. These questions can be found on page 178 of *The Creative Curriculum for Preschool*.

- In each interest area section of Chapter 4, there is section called "Using (name of interest area) to Teach Literacy Skills." Locate this section in your assigned interest area.

- This section gives specific examples of open-ended questions and comments you can use as children play with common classroom materials.

- Look in your interest area section to find an example of each type of question listed on the handout. Record the questions in the appropriate box.

Lead a discussion about the types of questions found in the examples:

- Did one type of question appear more often?

- Were there any types of questions that were missing?

- If so, how could you phrase that type of question as it relates to one of the materials in this section?

Distribute the materials for each interest area to the appropriate group. Have the participants develop each type of question based on the materials given to their group.

SUMMARY

Summarize the workshop:

- Asking open-ended questions encourages children to elaborate on their own ideas and communicate them with others.

- Open-ended questions help children to build vocabulary as well as language skills.

- It is important to use open-ended questions naturally and in response to what children are doing or saying. Overwhelming children with too many questions may discourage children from talking and responding.

NOTES

Building Language Using Open-Ended Questions

Type of Question	Examples from Chapter 4
To put thoughts into words Why do you think the little boy in the story was sad?	
To observe What do you see, hear, feel? What did you notice?	
To make predictions What do you think will happen if you keep adding blocks to your tower?	
To think about similarities and differences How are these two blocks the same? What makes these things go together?	
To apply knowledge to solve a problem What could you do to keep the paint from dripping on the floor?	
To stretch thinking What would happen if there were no cars, trucks, buses, planes, or boats? How would we get around?	
To consider consequences What would happen if you left your drawing outside and it rained?	
To evaluate What made you decide to pick this book to read? How did this make you feel?	
To assess feelings How would you feel if that happened to you?	

3L30

WORKSHOP

Using Assessment Information to Guide Literacy Learning

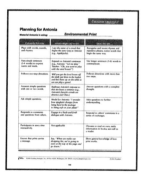

☐ Handout 3L31,
   p. 166–167
☐ Handout 3L31-Trainer,
   pp. 168–169
☐ Literacy materials (e.g.,
   books, environmental
   print, magnetic letters,
   writing materials, story
   props, etc.)
☐ *Literacy*, Appendix

PREPARATION

Duplicate the handout. Review the trainer's version of the handout in which environmental print is used as one example.

Gather literacy materials (books, story props, environmental print, writing materials, magnetic letters, chalkboards and chalk) and place them on each table. You will need at least one item for each pair of participants.

Review the Language Development objectives of the *Developmental Continuum* found in the Appendix of *Literacy: The Creative Curriculum Approach*.

INTRODUCTION

Introduce the workshop:

- Good teaching begins with observation.

- When you know a child's strengths, you can use this information to make informed decisions and guide learning.

- *The Developmental Continuum* helps you pinpoint a child's language and literacy development and provides useful information for instructional purposes.

- The Language Development section of the *Developmental Continuum* can be found in the Appendix of *Literacy: The Creative Curriculum Approach*.

- Three additional observation forms are included in the Appendix. These will enable you to make a more informed decision about where a child is on the *Developmental Continuum*.

ACTIVITY

Have participants work in pairs. Distribute the handout. Use the following points as you review it with the group.

- Assume that Antonia is a child in your class. Over the past several months, you have been observing Antonia and recording her progress on the *Developmental Continuum*.

- The first column of the handout summarizes where Antonia is on the *Developmental Continuum* in the area of language development.

- In the third column, are the next steps you hope she will achieve.

- Imagine that Antonia is using one of the materials you see on your table. Based on what you know about Antonia's language and literacy development, what can you say or do to help her progress?

- Brainstorm together and record your ideas in the middle column on the handout.

Use the suggestions on the Trainer's handout to help them get started. Have each pair share one or two strategies with others at their table or with the whole group. Add to their ideas as needed.

SUMMARY

Summarize the workshop:

- To help children progress in language and literacy development, teachers must be knowledgeable about what children already know and can do.

- In a *Creative Curriculum* classroom, the starting point is observation using *The Developmental Continuum* as a guide.

- *The Developmental Continuum* informs your teaching and helps you tailor the activities and experiences you offer to meet each child's unique strengths and needs.

VARIATION

Ask teachers to bring in assessment information (portfolios and reports in the area of language) for one child.

Have participants find a partner then give the following directions:

- Discuss each child's assessment information.

- Talk about each child's interests.

- Based on this information, identify some activities and experiences that will help each child progress on the *The Developmental Continuum*, objectives 38–50.

Planning for Antonia

Material Antonia is using: _____

Currently Antonia:	What I might say or do:	Soon she will ...
Plays with words, sounds, and rhymes.		Recognize and invent rhymes and repetitive phases; notice words that begin the same way.
Uses simple sentences (3–4 words) to express wants and needs.		Use longer sentences (5–6) words to communicate.
Follows two-step directions.		Follows directions with more than two steps.
Answers simple questions with one or two words.		Answer questions with a complete thought.
Ask simple questions.		Asks questions to further understanding.
Responds to comments and questions from others.		Respond to others' comments in a series of exchanges.
Participates in story time interactively.		Chooses to read on own; seeks information in books; sees self as a reader.
Knows that print carries a message.		Show general knowledge of how print works.

Planning for Antonia, continued

Material Antonia is using: _____

Currently Antonia:	What I might say or do:	Soon she will . . .
Recognizes and identifies a few letters by name.		Recognize and name many letters.
Uses illustrations to guess what the text says.		Make judgements about words and text by noticing features (other than letters or words).
Imitates act of reading in play.		Compare and predict story events.
Imitates act of writing in play.		Understand there is a way to write that conveys meaning.
Uses scribble writing and letter-like forms.		Write recognizable letters especially those in her own name.

Planning for Antonia

Material Antonia is using: _____ *Environmental Print*

Currently Antonia:	What I might say or do:	Soon she will ...
Plays with words, sounds, and rhymes.	*I spy the name of a cereal that begins the same way as Antonia (e.g., AppleJacks).*	Recognize and invent rhymes and repetitive phases; notice words that begin the same way.
Uses simple sentences (3–4 words) to express wants and needs.	*Expand on Antonia's sentences (e.g., Antonia: "Let me play." Teacher: "Oh, you want to play with the cereal boxes?")*	Use longer sentences (5–6) words to communicate.
Follows two-step directions.	*Will you get the food boxes off the shelf, put them in the basket, and line them up on the table so we can play a game?*	Follows directions with more than two steps.
Answers simple questions with one or two words.	*Rephrase Antonia's response so that she hears a sentence (e.g., Antonia's favorite cereals are Cheerios and Chex.)*	Answer questions with a complete thought.
Ask simple questions.	*Model for Antonia: "I wonder how spaghetti changes from being hard in the package to being soft on your plate?"*	Asks questions to further understanding.
Responds to comments and questions from others.	*Engage in a back-and-forth dialogue with Antonia.*	Respond to others' comments in a series of exchanges.
Participates in story time interactively.	*Not applicable*	Chooses to read on own; seeks information in books; sees self as a reader.
Knows that print carries a message.	*Say, "When we make our shopping list, we're going to start at the top of the page and go down."*	Show general knowledge of how print works.

©2005 Teaching Strategies, Inc., PO Box 42243, Washington, DC 20015; www.TeachingStrategies.com

3L31-Trainer

Planning for Antonia, continued

Material Antonia is using: _____ ***Environmental Print*** _____

Currently Antonia:	What I might say or do:	Soon she will ...
Recognizes and identifies a few letters by name.	*This ad for cantaloupe has some letters that are just like those in your name. Can you find them?*	Recognize and name many letters.
Uses illustrations to guess what the text says.	*Call Antonio's attention to features of words and text. "There are so many long words on this box, look at this one. It's even longer than your name."*	Make judgements about words and text by noticing features (other than letters or words).
Imitates act of reading in play.	*Not applicable*	Compare and predict story events.
Imitates act of writing in play.	*Can you make a shopping list so we know what to buy at the grocery store.*	Understand there is a way to write that conveys meaning.
Uses scribble writing and letter-like forms.	*Write alongside Antonia as she is making her grocery list. Call attention to letters and talk about how they are formed.*	Write recognizable letters especially those in her own name.

WORKSHOPS

🔑 Key Points	⊛ Workshop	🗒 Materials	🕐 Time (minutes)
When children investigate a topic, they can apply literacy skills they have acquired and learn new skills. All the components of literacy can be addressed in a study.	**Integrating Literacy Into Content Area Studies** (p. 172)	☐ *Literacy*, pp. 127–131 ☐ Chart paper, markers	45–60

WORKSHOP

Integrating Literacy Into Content Area Studies

☐ *Literacy*, pp. 127–131
☐ Chart paper, markers

PREPARATION

This workshop is appropriate for participants who are knowledgeable about how to implement studies in their classrooms.

Write each of the following headings on a separate piece of chart paper:

Water
Our Class Pet
Balls
Clothing
Homes
Gardening
Our Building
Cars
The Cafeteria
Musical Instruments
Wheels

Have one sheet prepared for each table. (Note: you may not need to use all of these topics.)

INTRODUCTION

Introduce the workshop:

- In previous workshops, you learned about the research-based components of a comprehensive literacy program, the skills children need to be successful readers and writers, and the teaching strategies teachers use to help children develop these skills.

- Research on literacy learning also indicates that children need frequent opportunities to read and write in ways that are interesting and motivating.

- The purpose of this workshop is to illustrate how studies offer a meaningful and engaging context for children to learn and use important literacy skills.

Have participants read "Studies, Using Literacy to Learn," on pages 127–131 of *Literacy: The Creative Curriculum Approach*.

Next, have participants work with others at their tables to identify some key characteristics of the flower study. Also have them note how literacy was addressed in the study.

Record their ideas on a chart or transparency.

Possible responses:

The study began with an ordinary moment (e.g., children bringing in flowers from the playground).

The teacher probed to find out children's questions.

Finding answers to children's questions was the focus of the study.

Children used literacy skills in meaningful ways to help them find answers to their questions.

Children were motivated to learn.

Children were reading and writing for a purpose.

Make the following points:

- *Creative Curriculum* teachers offer children opportunities to study topics that are interesting and meaningful to them.

- Through studies, teachers can integrate content (literacy, math, science, social studies, the arts, and technology) and address developmental goals.

◀ ACTIVITY

Explain to participants that they will participate in an activity called "carousel brainstorming" in which they will generate a list of ways literacy can be used to help children learn more about a topic.

Place one labeled chart face down on each table. Describe the process:

- Select a recorder for your group.

- Each group will have one minute to brainstorm a list of ways literacy can be used to help children learn more about the topic of study recorded at the top of your paper.

- When time is up, rotate the charts clockwise.

- You will have a minute to review the list.

- After I give the signal to begin, you may add your ideas.

Rotate the charts in one-minute intervals until each group receives its original chart.

Have the participants review the final chart to see the variety of literacy experiences listed.

Next, have participants analyze the activities and experiences as they relate to the seven literacy components (literacy as a source of enjoyment; vocabulary and language; phonological awareness; knowledge of print; letters and words; comprehension; books and other texts) and the teaching strategies (talking, singing, and playing with language; reading aloud; storytelling; story retelling; writing; playing) to determine if they were addressed or used. Participants may either color code the activities or write abbreviations next to the activities.

Have each group give a report; or, ask each group to post its chart on the wall and allow time for participants to walk about and review them.

Invite participants to share their observations about the experience (e.g., some components were addressed more often; one or more strategies were seldom used).

SUMMARY

Summarize the workshop:

- A central goal of a *Creative Curriculum* program is to help children see themselves as readers and writers rather than to teach isolated literacy skills.

- When children use literacy in meaningful, purposeful ways during studies, they have the opportunity to practice many skills and become more proficient in using them.

NOTES

NOTES

NOTES

NOTES

NOTES

NOTES

NOTES

NOTES

NOTES

NOTES